THE EXPERT GUIDE
to WINNING
SWEEPSTAKES

Sweepstakes, Contests, Games & Prize Promotion Handbook

JEFFREY FEINMAN *&* JOHN MINGES

www.SweepstakesExpert.com

The Expert Guide to Winning Sweepstakes:
Sweepstakes, Contests, Games & Prize Promotion Handbook

ISBN: 978-0-9905990-1-2

Cover and interior designed by Stephanie W. Dicken

Special thanks to our editor Dr. Virginia Hardy as well as Gwen Beauchamp for her assistance.

Table of Contents

Preface

One of the biggest challenges in writing any book on the topic of sweepstakes is making sure you thoroughly cover the basics for the beginner while providing new information for those individuals who would be considered long time pros. This by far is the most difficult task to accomplish.

With this in mind we begin by giving readers the history of sweepstakes and then quickly progress to understanding all the complexities of not only entering sweepstakes but being successful as well. Both beginners and advanced sweepers will be intrigued and (we hope) impressed at the depth of knowledge we share concerning all aspects of the sweepstakes and promotional business. The pages contained within are not filled with fluff but come from decades of involvement in the industry.

We invite you to join us on this journey of learning what it takes to become a professional sweepstakes aficionado.

Introduction

Anyone can enter sweepstakes, right? Well, yes as long as you qualify, but understanding what it takes to win is much more of a difficult process that will be explained in greater detail as you digest the contents of this book. Your travel through the land of sweepstakes doesn't have to be a frustrating one. Having a trusted expert guide with a map in hand who can show you the way should not only be helpful but profitable as well. Are you ready to win?

In preparation for writing this book, countless hours have been spent reading, researching and reviewing dozens of books related to this topic that have been written within the last 20 years. The information you are about to receive comes from actual life experiences not just book knowledge of parroting back the same old stories told by others. By far the biggest difference between this book and all the rest is that the information we share comes from actual industry experiences. Both authors have been directly involved in all aspects of sales, promotions and, yes, sweepstakes! We are certain some of those nagging questions you've always had about sweepstakes will finally be answered. Also, we will likely dispel some common myths. By the time you finish this book we are certain that you will learn some new tips that will enable you to win more while losing less. We realize your time is valuable, so let's begin.

Skeptics and Believers

Are sweepstakes really legitimate? Does someone really win the prizes? Don't the prizes go to friends of the judging organizations? The answers are: Yes. Yes. No.

The great American dream has always been to strike it rich fast. That's the story of Columbus who, looking for spices and tea, accidently found a continent. It's the story of the California Gold Rush that lured thousands of people westward to pan for gold. It's the story of the Texas oil wells. An accident. A miracle. A gushing black fountain in your own backyard. Somewhere each of us, deep in our heart of hearts, has a secret wish to win big and become a millionaire.

But let's be honest, few of us know how to go about it. Have you ever entered a contest or a sweepstakes? Have you ever bought a chance in a lottery? Have you ever played bingo and won? Maybe you have – once. Or twice. Or, maybe you've never entered at all, never tried your luck, never played to win.

Along with the dream comes the suspicion, "Oh, I could never win." Or, "Why should I bother? Everybody knows you lose. It's a waste of my time or perhaps a waste of postage." Or, "They aren't legitimate. The winners are friends of the judges." Or, "Nobody wins. I never knew anybody to win. They never give away real prizes."

⌐able that people are generally skeptical. It
⌐ minds around the fact that companies
⌐s that give away prizes, sometimes of great
⌐dividuals who abide by the official rules in order to
⌐y to win. But this fact is true and each year in the United
States millions of dollars in cash, cars, and other merchandise
are given away. Best of all, these prizes are given away to people
just like you.

This book will tell you how you can get your fair share.

The World of Promotions

Basically, the whole concept of promotion is to offer something
that consumers do not expect in the normal course of doing business.
But the narrower topic of prize promotion adds the element of
gratification to the unexpected. It presents the consumer with the
opportunity to win a prize for performing some particular process.
In many cases that involves providing certain basic information
so you can be contacted in the event you win. Prize offers are
based on a basic principle of psychology - the modeling effect
related to positive reinforcement - in which the subject experiences
a certain pleasurable consequence following the performance
of a specific task. Although most people will lose, the entrant
is having a positive experience because he is modeling behavior
after individuals he knows have won prizes. Prize promotions
continue to be an integral part of most major corporate marketing
strategies. With every passing year you are likely to see an increase,
not only in the *number* of promotions, but in the various *types* and
users of promotions. The major reasons for this phenomenon is
most likely due to the fact that products and marketing have gone
through several stages in their development.

In the first stage, before the turn of the century, a product
was simply sold on its superiority. An individual was capable of
making a superb wooden bowl or a magnificent horseshoe, or

individuals were known far and wide for their unique sewing skills, and so the sale of a product was based on its quality or perceived quality.

With the Industrial Revolution it became possible for mass manufacturers to create products of equal quality. A good organic chemist with $200 could figure out the formula for any of the various medicines or cleaning products. Anyone who had the financial resources to invest in machinery was capable of producing a competitive product. Therefore, product superiority diminished. Except for products that were protected by patents, the age of product superiority was over.

In the second stage, in the development of marketing, marketers began to ask, "How do we differentiate our product from all the others on the shelves that are of equal quality? How can we cut it in the marketplace?" The answer was ADVERTISING superiority. The manufacturer used advertising to create a unique position for its product. Companies turned to advertising as a response to parity products. If all products were essentially the same, then the secret was to make them *appear* different in the mind of the consumer. Fab™ and Tide™ were chemically the same, but the creative imagination of the advertising community could instill a difference in the consumer's mind. Although Camel™, Lucky Strike™, and Old Gold™ were essentially the same tobacco product, creative advertising convinced the consumer that there were wide differences between them. Consumers were essentially buying advertising, not the products.

By the 1960s, when most advertising seemed to be taking on similar characteristics, we were entering stage three. We were fast approaching parity advertising. Many advertisers had found new and exciting ways to extol the virtues of their products. Then, all of a sudden, there was a formula for good advertisements, and everyone knew the elements that a successful ad must contain. If you had examined ads for a dozen different dog foods, you would have seen a striking similarity among them - dogs running and jumping, their tails wagging as they raced to the bowl of dog food. It became apparent that just as there were few unique products, there were few unique advertising campaigns.

When advertising of cigarettes was first allowed they all depicted the same thing - a good-looking man in the great outdoors or at a post party enjoying a cigarette. So now, in this third stage in the development of product marketing, we have advertising clutter. As each of the marketing disciplines evolved, they all reached a clutter level. Regardless of how good your product may be, there are probably many others just as worthy. All are attractively packaged. All are attractively and expensively advertised.

Now that we have product parity *and* advertising parity, what's next? How do you create a demonstrable difference for your product? With PROMOTION superiority - prize promotion in particular. Prize promotions are capable of differentiating products *and* advertising by giving the consumer "something extra." So when people go to the supermarket and see endless rolls of paper towels each one screaming "New, Blue, and Improved!" - it is the one that says "WIN $25,000! Free Game Ticket Inside" that catches the consumer's attention.

Prize promotions were once the exclusive provinces of the packaged goods and food market industries. Today, anyone can effectively apply the chance to win a valuable prize - the chance to win a dream. The prize promotion can be the solution to almost any business problem that requires a specific consumer action. Fundraisers use sweepstakes, and so do airlines, soft drink bottlers, newspapers, and broadcasters. In fact, there is hardly a business you can think of that has not used prize promotions successfully. In fact, prize promotions are so ubiquitous today that they range in the thousands each month. That means thousands of chances for you to win!

The History of Prize Promotion

It was P.T. Barnum, appropriately, who conducted the first recorded contest in the United States. In 1850, he offered a $200 prize for a song, "Ode to America" - written to promote "The Swedish Nightingale," Jenny Lind. In 1897, Eastman Kodak held a photography contest to increase public interest in picture-taking. But to trace the evolution of lotteries and, later prize promotions, we have to go back to biblical times.

"LOT" - Its Original Definition and Derivation

The word *lot* originated from the Teutonic root *hleut*. It was used to describe an object, such as a disk, pebble, or bean, which was either cast or drawn to make some sort of decision (often disputes over division of land or goods). It was believed that these decisions were made under Divine Guidance.

In English, the word *hlot* or *hlodd* evolved into the lot in the 13th century. In Dutch, it was *lot*; in Danish, *lod*; in Swedish, *lott*; and in Icelandic, *hlautr*. The Romance languages adopted the Teutonic word, and it became *lot* in French, *lote* in Portuguese, *loto* in Spanish, and *lotto* in Italian. Scholars differ on how the English word lottery was derived. Some believe it came from the Italian *lotteria*, while others say it came from Flanders' *lotterie*.

The Bible

Whatever its derivation, evidence of lotteries is found as early as Old Testament times. The use of the lot is reported throughout the Bible. Lots were used to decide everything from the division of land to political and labor issues.

The instances of lots described in the Bible are staggering in number and type. The first King of Israel was chosen by lot. Leviticus 16:8 states: "And Aaron shall cast lots upon the two goats; one lot for the Lord, and the other lot for the scapegoat." In the book of Numbers we find that allocation of land was determined by chance. It is written there that after taking a census of the Israelites, Moses apportioned the land west of the Jordan "for an inheritance according to the number of names" to each tribe (Numbers 26:55). In order to avoid jealousy, the territories were divided by lot.

Distribution of unpleasant duties were also decided by lot. In Jonah 1:7, ancient sailors frightened by the tempest cast lots to choose the party that would sail, and "The lot fell upon Jonah." Legal controversies were also settled by lot. "The Lot causeth contentions to cease and parteth between the mighty" (Joshua 7:16). Lots were also recommended by Solomon as a method of settling disputes.

The New Testament

The proliferation of the use of lots continues in the New Testament. Divine will was ascertained by the casting of lots. Stones of different colors or inscribed with symbols were put into a vessel that was then shaken until one of the stones popped out. People believed that this method of selection removed any human element and that the choice was made by God. After the death of Judas Iscariot, the casting of lots was used to choose his successor as an apostle-either Joseph or Matthias. "And they prayed and said, 'Lord...show which one of these two Thou has chosen to take the place in this ministry...,' And they cast lots...and the lots fell on Matthias." (Acts 1:24,26)

The Romans

The Romans continued the use of lotteries as a method of predicting events. Sortes-rods or plates bearing inscriptions were drawn. The interpretation of the inscription provided answers to questions on a wide variety of subjects. A forerunner of present-day lotteries, the questioner paid an oracle to draw the sortes. Cicero (106-43 B.C.) renounced these drawings saying, "The whole scheme of divination by lots was fraudulently contrived from mercenary motives as a means of encouraging superstition and error."

At the lavish banquets of the day, the Roman emperors distributed gifts to their guests using lots to determine who would get what. Elagabulus distributed chances inscribed on spoons at his feasts and games. The inscriptions determined the utility and value of the gift that would go to the bearer of that spoon. A guest might receive something as valuable as 10 pounds of gold or 10 camels, or as useless as 10 flies!

Augustus gave his followers gifts by selling them lots. The articles represented by these lots were a mystery in addition to being of unequal value. Everyone was required to buy a lot and run the risk of loss or gain. This proceeding, with equal payments and unequal prizes or no prize at all, parallels the lotteries in Europe and North America in the 17th and 18th centuries.

There is evidence that the first lottery used to sell goods took place in Rome. Italian merchants were said to keep an "Urn of Fortune" from which their customers were permitted to draw a ticket inscribed with the names of various articles. The customers then drew another ticket inscribed with a price. The holder of the ticket was thus entitled to the merchandise inscribed on the first ticket at the price stated on the second.

The Greeks

In other references of this period, the *Iliad* notes that Greek heroes marked their own lots and cast them to determine who would have the honor of fighting Hector. In the first century, Tacitus records that Teutonic tribes practiced divination and wizardry using lots to decide whether a battle should be fought, and to determine the leaders and the fate of prisoners. The drawing of lots was also used to determine the answers to questions such as: Who shall be sacrificed for food? Who will do battle? and Who is guilty of a crime? The answers to such questions, as well as anything determined by lot, were not subject to argument. The decision was final.

Medieval Period

In the medieval period - from 1443 to 1449 - there is evidence of lotteries in places such as Oudenarde, Utrecht, Ghent, Bruges, and L'Ecluse where the earliest recorded lottery of this period took place. Its purpose was to raise 10,000 salut d'or for construction of walls and fortifications.

In 1446, English and Scottish names were found among the participants in Brugeouis lotteries. This is particularly interesting because it shows that over a century before lotteries appeared in Britain, chances were known to Englishmen.

In the first half of the 16th century, there are records of numerous lotteries held in territories now known as Holland, Belgium, and France. In 1526, an edict was handed down forbidding all unlicensed lotteries, with a penalty of confiscation of prizes and all money received. This is probably an early step in the evolution of state lotteries.

England

Although the earliest record of an English lottery was the one held by Queen Elizabeth in 1568, historians believe that lotteries took place earlier. An example may be a lottery chartered in 1566 to raise funds to repair harbors. However, lotteries were not used extensively in England until the 17th century when they became a public nuisance; they were suppressed in 1699. The suppression of these private ventures paved the way for all kinds of state lotteries, which continued for about 130 years until they were abolished in 1826.

While important public works were funded with lotteries, abuses in the system, such as gambling on chances, are to blame for lotteries' fall from grace. Despite this, many lotteries (under names like art unions, sweepstakes, subscription funds, ballots, and tombolas) were held with or without official sanction.

Earliest Lotteries Held Elsewhere

In 1470, in Augsburg in the ancient duchy of Bavaria, a lottery was held that sold 36,000 tickets. While there is evidence of lotteries held at L'Ecluse and Lille in the 15th century, the lottery was formally introduced into France in 1533 by the Italians. These lotteries were known as blanques (in Italian, bianca) simply because white tickets outnumbered black tickets. In 1659, at the time of the marriage of Louise XIV, French state lotteries were organized. These continue today as an aid to France's financial resources.

In Italy, the earliest documented lottery took place in Florence in 1530. A new kind of lottery was introduced by a Genoese senate member in 1623 and was known as the famous "groco del lotto."

North America

The Virginia Lotteries of 1611 are the first known lotteries in North America. Experiencing difficulty in supporting its settlement in Jamestown, the Virginia Company of London petitioned the king for relief. This merchant group was granted a charter in 1612 to conduct one or more lotteries in England within a year's time. Continued permission after that year was at the discretion of the king.

In an early use of advertising, a ballad was written to stir up enthusiasm for the lottery. "London's Lotterie" was sung to the tune of "Lusty Gallant" and proclaimed the need for colonization of the future United States. It appealed to both patriotism and religion, all while stressing the value of prizes.

In 1619, complaints began to surface that the lottery had demoralized business and industry. A year later, with little warning, the Privy Council halted the lotteries. Another reason for the ban was discord among officers of the Virginia Company itself with accusations that money was misappropriated. Whatever the reasons, the ban was a tremendous blow for the Virginia Company and its struggling colony in America.

In the American colonies, lotteries soon became a part of everyday life. Many reasons account for the lottery's acceptance in the newly formed America: the prevalence and popularity of lotteries in the Old World, economic pressures associated with establishment of government and cities, and a general lack of moral opposition to lotteries. All of these reasons stimulated the already recognized and accepted gambling instinct.

In America, as in England, lotteries fell into two categories: drawings by individuals for personal profit and drawings legally sanctioned for public benefit. The official attitude toward lotteries proceeded through four stages:

1. Lassiez-faire.
2. Legal sanctions for some drawings and no restrictions on others.
3. Outlawing unauthorized lotteries.
4. Total prohibition.

Lotteries were often used to dispose of household goods or land because it was an assured way of getting a fair price. Even Thomas Jefferson wrote approvingly of lotteries used for these purposes. For the most part, such lotteries were conducted with the public interest in mind. The funds raised were used to build bridges, churches, schools, and roads. One of the most famous lotteries of the time was in Pennsylvania and raised money for the "College, Academy and Charitable School of Philadelphia," now known as the University of Pennsylvania.

As could have been expected, when lotteries became popular, their sponsors and promoters were often found to be acting in bad faith. Corrupt promoters sometimes fixed lotteries so that tickets for the most valuable prizes were never drawn, or they used inferior merchandise for the majority of the prizes. It was not unusual for a promoter to disappear with the proceeds without even holding his drawing.

Merchants of the day opposed lotteries because they saw them as competition. Money used to purchase lottery tickets might otherwise have been used to buy goods or services. But for the most part, the public was indifferent. The Society of Friends was the only group to consistently oppose lotteries. The Quakers' disapproval of all types of gambling, and many forms of amusement in general, accounts for their opposition. However, at that time the Quakers were not a large group and their opinion had little effect on lotteries.

Nonetheless, lotteries were eventually widely banned. As cited by governments of the day, the main reason for banning unlicensed lotteries was because of the effect they had on the poor. Apparently all forms of gambling had a particular appeal to the lower classes.

Eventually, local governments considered regulating lotteries rather than banning them altogether. New York, Massachusetts, Connecticut, Rhode Island, and Pennsylvania were among the first states to prohibit lotteries that didn't have legislative approval. Virginia's legislation came much later than the other colonies. The reason for Virginia's tolerance was perhaps due to the fact that several eminent figures were often associated with lotteries - George Washington, to name one.

Why were lotteries licensed rather than abolished altogether? The main reason seems to be that the people wanted these drawings. They believed they could be conducted honestly and felt it was an individual's business how he risked his money. Also, there was a high degree of financial instability in the provinces at the time. Funds were needed to finance wars with the French and the Indians. There was also an unfavorable balance of trade with England. Lotteries were viewed as a viable solution to all these problems.

There was a set method for operations of lotteries in early America:

1. A group or individual would petition the General Assembly to obtain permission to conduct a lottery.

2. After authorizing the lottery, the legislature would give the group a set of rules to follow for the operation of the lottery.

3. Appointments of directors and managers were made.

4. Managers were bonded to protect against fraud.

5. Numbered lottery tickets were produced in triplicate: one for the purchaser (signed by the seller), one sealed in a box, and the third kept in a ticket book used for comparison if a mistake occurred or fraud were suspected.

6. The drawing took place in a public room conducted by the managers. The sealed box containing the tickets was opened; the contents were mixed; and a person unconnected with the lottery drew the winning tickets.

7. A drawing was made from a second box containing tickets imprinted with a description of a prize and others that were blank. If the second ticket drawn was imprinted, then the holder of a numbered ticket was a winner.

Many schools of the day sought the use of lotteries for fundraising. King's College in New York, today known as Columbia University, was the first college granted a license to raise funds by lottery. The first lottery of any kind to be approved by the Connecticut Assembly was for the benefit of Yale. In an unusual example, the College of New Jersey, not Princeton University, was refused the right to hold a lottery by the New Jersey legislators. The college then petitioned Connecticut for a license to hold the lottery in that state. In 1753, the Connecticut Assembly granted the license; the drawing was held in Stamford and raised 7,500 pounds. Princeton was not permitted to hold a lottery in New Jersey until 1762, nearly 10 years later.

Harvard College was not as successful in its use of a lottery. The college received legislative approval in 1765, but the financial situation in Massachusetts was in great turmoil and residents had little money to spend on lotteries.

At about the same time, as early as 1761, the British government was not favorably disposed to colonial lotteries. In 1769, a letter was sent to the governors of Delaware, Georgia, Massachusetts, New Hampshire, New Jersey, New York, North Carolina, Pennsylvania, South Carolina, and West Florida that in essence directed them not to authorize any lottery without the express permission of the crown. So, for a number of years after this edict was handed down, the only colonies that conducted lotteries were Rhode Island, Maryland, and Connecticut.

After 1789, lotteries reached their greatest period of popularity. In the late 1700s, America experienced enormous growth, which in turn led to increasing demands from American citizens. There were roads, canals, and bridges to be built, and sewage and transportation systems to be developed. By this time lotteries were a strong part of the country's economy; they were a proven method of raising funds to meet all these new demands. All was well with the lottery system, but it would not last for long.

As the lotteries increased, there was a growing need for lottery contractors and ticket brokers. The people who assumed these functions were those who recognized the tremendous opportunities the lottery system offered. These people often exploited this system for personal gain.

Ticket brokers of the day relieved lottery managers of the task of selling tickets. They usually purchased larger numbers of tickets at a discount and then sold them at their original price. Eventually, the tickets were sold exclusively at the broker's place of business, usually in shops and in branches across the country.

For a fee, lottery contractors assumed control of the entire operation of a lottery including the drawing. Contractors used brokers as outlets for the sale of lottery tickets. This led to the birth of big business. Business concerns of all types used the successful techniques developed by lottery contractors and profited greatly from them. In fact, the lottery gave rise to private banking and later to stock brokerages. Some of the country's largest banking institutions were founded by lottery contractors and brokers. The First National Bank of New York City, chartered in 1863 and now known as Citibank, and the Chase National Bank, chartered in 1873, were both founded by John Thompson, a former lottery broker.

"Insurance," a practice used widely by the middle of the 19th century, was meant to aid individuals who couldn't afford the price of a lottery ticket. This practice became one of the most lucrative parts of a ticket agent's business and subsequently, the subject of severe criticism. The "insurance" business required the new practice of extending a drawing over a period of several weeks. A fixed number of tickets were drawn each day, and, as time passed, people began to speculate as to when undrawn numbers would be chosen. Ticket brokers took advantage of this speculation by accepting bets on which numbers would be selected the following day. Newspapers printed the "insurance rates," or odds, on a daily basis. Smart lottery players soon found that they could not lose if they took part in the insurance scheme. For example, an individual holding a lottery ticket that was yet undrawn could bet his ticket was one of the many blank ones sold. When the ticket was drawn and turned out to be a prize winning ticket, he of course received the prize on the ticket. But even if the ticket were a blank, the holder was a winner because he had "insured" his investment in the lottery ticket.

As might be expected, "insurance" practices led to many abuses of the lottery system. It did not take long for the governments of various states to take remedial action. By 1840, 12 states had anti-lottery legislation, while over the next 20 years additional states, including Maryland, Alabama, and New Jersey, outlawed lotteries altogether.

Meanwhile, the Louisiana lottery came through this rough period of regulation virtually unscathed. All through the 1880s, the Louisiana lottery was subjected to challenges by the courts and the legislature, and yet it somehow survived this onslaught. The staying power of this lottery led to accusations that legislators accepted bribes to vote in favor of individual lottery schemes.

The unsavory situation in Louisiana was not typical of other states. In 1878, anti-lottery bills began to be introduced in Congress. Eventually, even Louisiana was the victim of this rampant opposition to lotteries.

President Harrison was one of the first public figures of this time to express the sentiment of the public when he denounced lotteries, saying that they "debauched and defrauded" the people of the United States. In 1890, he asked Congress for severe legislation that would curb lotteries. Two years later, Congress passed a bill that prohibited the use of the mails for the purposes of lottery. It is not surprising that this bill made it through Congress since all but 2 of the 44 states had already banned lottery activity in whole or in part. Aside from the rampant exploitation of privately sponsored lotteries, a major reason behind the anti-lottery legislation was the potential use of lotteries to produce revenue for the government. Thus, we witness the birth of the state-run lottery.

The anti-lottery laws of the 1930s and 40s limited the use of chance in prize promotions conducted by marketers of that era. Therefore, the contest of skill, which eliminated chance, became the most prevalent type of prize promotion. After a time, state legislators began to realize that sweepstakes and other types of prize promotions were not being run like lotteries or any form of gambling, and restrictions on their use were relaxed.

In the 1960s many forms of prize promotion grew increasingly popular. However, this burgeoning popularity came to an abrupt halt after investigations held in 1968 by the Federal Trade Commission and Congress revealed abuses within the prize promotion industry. It wasn't until the late 1970s that prize promotion regained its former stature in the marketing industry. With the advent of state lotteries, legislation governing prize promotion cleared the way for a resurgence of its former popularity. It wasn't that long ago, however, that the most popular way a person could enter a promotion was by filling out an entry pad at a local establishment and dropping his/her entry into a box hoping it might be drawn. Eventually mailing in entry forms became an option. Today things have changed. Technology has produced and continues to develop multiple methods of communication that most corporations seek to capitalize on allowing them to expand their ability to connect with current and hopefully new consumers. Individuals now have more ways to enter their beloved sweepstakes than ever before. Text to enter, Tweet to enter, post on various social media websites to enter. The list of ways to "connect" appears to be growing each year. Of course mail-in entries via a postcard or first class letter are still acceptable in some sweepstakes but it appears this once favored means of entry is slowly becoming obsolete.

State Lotteries - Today

There are a total of 44 states as well as the District of Columbia, Puerto Rico, and the US Virgin Islands that have lotteries. The six states that don't have lotteries are Alabama, Mississippi, Utah, Alaska, Hawaii, and Nevada. All 44 states offer both Powerball™ and Mega Millions™ which help create the massive size jackpots that are paid out. The odds of winning the Powerball™ jackpot are extremely small at one in 292 million while the odds of winning the Mega Million™ jackpot are approximately one in 259 million.

States use the monies collected to pay for a wide range of programs it otherwise would have to use tax dollars to fund. Some of the programs include education, programs for seniors, economic development and much more. So far the biggest jackpot in US history was paid in January 2016 in the amount of $1.5 billion that was split three ways to winners in California, Florida and Tennessee. Tickets can be purchased at many retail establishments.

Second Chance - Lottery Drawings

State lotteries understand that the vast majority of players are losers so in an effort to take the sting out of losing, many states have created separate second chance drawings. Individuals are allowed to use both scratch off tickets as well as all the other printed game tickets like Powerball™ and Mega Millions™. To enter, some states have developed an app where you can use your smart phone to instantly scan the ticket bar code or enter the code manually. Typically, you are given a point value equal to one point per dollar. These points can then be used to enter either weekly or monthly second chance drawings. The odds of winning these drawing are also very slim but again it gives the consumer extra value for their purchase. Many people are unaware these second chance drawings exist.

Another point that is important to make is that you should save your losing tickets. Why, you might ask? Well, if you win and receive a 1099 Form that you are required to file with your federal taxes, the law allows you to deduct any loses against your wins. Having the losing tickets will help in proving those losses in the event you get audited.

Prize Promotions - A Brief Overview

It is important that you understand some of the basics concerning prize promotions. In general, these fall into several distinct categories: lotteries, sweepstakes and contests. There are also games and bingo which we will briefly highlight.

A lottery has the elements of prize, chance, and consideration present. Lotteries are legal only when conducted by a state government. Usually, the prizes are monetary. Of course, the element of chance is the fact that you have a chance or opportunity to win. The consideration is the money that you spend to buy a lottery ticket.

There has been a tremendous growth in lotteries in the last decade, but it is worth noting that lotteries are strictly illegal when run by individuals or companies. In the United States, there is no national lottery at this time.

Sweepstakes promotions are typically offered by a company but can also be offered by individuals. In order to not be deemed an illegal lottery one of the elements, i.e. prize, chance or consideration must be eliminated for the promotion to be legal. Obviously, eliminating the prize would defeat the purpose that gives excitement to the promotion so in most cases the element of consideration is eliminated. On the surface, this might sound simple but it can indeed be very complex and where many sweepstakes tend to go awry.

Consideration by the simplest of definitions means the person entering the sweepstakes is not required to purchase any goods or services or provide any other monetary payment in order to enter. The act of consideration takes an even broader meaning today than just payment of monies, including requiring certain performances before a person is allowed to enter. This threshold can be crossed if the promotion requires the entrant to spend a substantial amount of effort and/ or time before an entry is allowed. Likewise, if the promotion requires the entrant to visit a store for the exclusive purpose of entering a sweepstakes or requires a receipt showing a proof of purchase then this could be deemed consideration. Another breach of consideration occurs when individuals are required to take long surveys before being allowed to enter. In general, courts have held that a "free" entry cannot be unduly burdensome whereby requiring individuals to do something they would not otherwise do. Consideration also can take place when the sponsor of the sweepstakes is shown to receive a benefit due to the efforts made by the entrant.

With this as your backdrop, you now can understand that in order for the consideration to truly be removed, the promoter must do more than just print the words: "no purchase is necessary", but the sponsor of the sweepstakes must provide an alternative method of entry where all entrants are given an equal chance also known as "equal dignity" of winning the prize or prizes offered.

Another type of prize promotion that you should know about is those known as contests. Here the element of chance is not present. In this prize format consideration is required, and it can be the purchase of the product. However, the element of chance is removed and substituted with skill. The skill factor must be quite real and not just a subterfuge. Unless you are a mathematician, guessing the number of beans in a jar is not skill. Unless you are a professional handicapper, guessing the score in advance of an athletic competition is not a skill.

The majority of contests of skill involve either writing a jingle, solving a puzzle, writing a 25-word statement, completing a rhyme, taking a photograph, or creating a recipe. However, contests could involve most any judgeable skill. Contests have asked for writing a complete novel to developing a product formula. For each one of these contests a rigid criteria for judging is established and the potential contestant is informed of these criteria in advance. These criteria might include originality, appropriateness, and creativity. Ties are not permitted in a contest of skill because there would then have to be duplicate prizes, so rules are established weighting the criteria. For instance, originality might count 50 percent, while appropriateness might be weighted at only 10 percent. Another method for breaking ties is by using second and third rounds - and more if necessary - of tiebreaking questions. Tiebreakers must be the same types as the original contest. For example, you cannot follow up a jingle-writing contest of skill with a tiebreaker that requires solving a puzzle. In many cases the winner is chosen by either a judging agency or the company directly administrating the promotion. Again, this is all based on the demonstrated talent or ability to accomplish the required task outlined in the official rules.

Games are yet another type of promotion commonly conducted by large corporations. Two recent examples include both McDonald's® and Subway®. These promotions tend to work best when store locations are either nationwide or within a specific geographic region of the country. Games typically offer consumers some type of ticket and no purchase is necessary to obtain such a ticket. Tickets may be matched for prizes or could offer the chance for instant win prizes.

Finally, an additional type of prize promotion is bingo. Bingo games are usually run by religious or charitable organizations. In New York City and other parts of the country there are actually special halls devoted to bingo. They are rented out by these organizations for a certain period of time, but most people who go to play bingo don't care in the least who's running the play operation. They simply want to play and win.

Why Do Companies Run Sweepstakes?

Each year, thousands upon thousands of people receive a letter or email that says, "Congratulations, you're the winner of a . . . prize offer." Hopefully, you have received such a correspondence at one time or another. And if you are a novice in entering sweepstakes, then you are probably curious why any company would want to do such a thing.

Why do companies run prize promotions? Why does the church run bingo games? Why do most states run lotteries? In short, the ultimate answer in all cases is the same. To make money.

In the case of the lottery, this answer seems to make the most sense. You pay to enter a lottery. You pay for each chance you take, each ticket that you obtain. States profits 40 to 50 percent per ticket sold. The rest of the money goes to pay for prizes.

If you play bingo, of course, you pay for the chance to win. Usually you must pay for each card that you play. If you play one game and use five cards, you must pay for each of those cards. Again, it's obvious how the church or other sponsoring organization makes money.

No doubt the free sweepstakes still leaves a rather large question in your mind. It's too much like the old American saying, "you don't get something for nothing." How can the manufacturers afford to give away prizes without directly requesting you buy their product or service? Well, indirectly they do. That's all any advertisement is-an indirect request to buy.

Major companies consider the price of sweepstakes prizes as simply another advertising cost. The sweepstakes attracts attention to a product or service. American marketers have discovered that the chance of winning turns on consumers and creates a good deal of involvement and excitement. They have found that by running a sweepstakes offer in an ad that the advertising relationship of that ad will increase. Everyone may be suspicious of getting something for nothing but secretly everyone wants to believe it. Everyone wants to be a winner. Everyone reads the ads that promise prizes.

One national magazine that runs sweepstakes feels that properly run promotions are as good for them as they are for the readers. They say that the sweepstakes is merely a device to attract attention to their magazine and the various other products they have to offer. For the reader, of course, there's the pleasure of playing the game and the possibility of winning many valuable prizes.

The sweepstakes is a great advertising tool, and it's good for you to know this, simply from the standpoint of being a potential winner. This doesn't mean that you'll be asked to say anything nice about the company or its products if you win. You might ask, "Will the company use my name in future advertisements?" One national company answers firmly, "No, not without your permission." Some promoters may have the secret hope that you'll be inclined to say a few nice words, but most, virtually all, won't ask for anything like that.

In the final analysis, the company doesn't really care who gets the prize. All they are interested in is the hoopla that the promotion creates. In the mind of the company, the prize promotion is frequently over long before the closing date. In other words, long before the drawings, long before the prizes are given away, the sweepstakes ad has run its course, and another product or service has made its debut.

Thus, when any company large or small runs a sweepstakes promotion all they really care about is that the promotion helps build consumer excitement and brand awareness and ultimately increase sales of their product or service.

The Love Hate Relationship

Those who enter sweepstakes with a passion proudly accept the title of being called "sweepers" or if you reside in the UK "compers" short for competitions.

But, let's be totally honest, not all sponsors running brand promotions necessarily enjoy our enthusiasm. Some, but not all companies, are concerned that the goal of hard core sweepers or compers is only winning the prize(s). Sponsors run sweepstakes in an effort to increase brand loyalty. A level of frustration can arise when marketing departments find that the contact information they receive actually comes from mostly disinterested parties.

Not all things are negative. However, the passionate sweepers who are very serious about the hobby do several things that could improve the promotion. First, the number of entries is definitely increased. Sweepers read the rules and figure out how many times they can enter and do so as often as possible. Second, the community of sweepstakes followers is huge and the networks for sharing information is vast so this will increase the awareness of the promotion exponentially. Brands like when their promotions go viral, no matter how it happens!

Next, those who have sweeping in their blood are quick to contact judging agencies and sponsors when something is wrong. Maybe the rules aren't clear, or they are contradictory. The application running the entry form shows an error code or the website itself is down. Generally the first person to notify the companies running promotions of these types of issues is likely a hard core sweeper.

Finally, companies need to understand winners actually help create brand loyalty. Marketing experts all agree that word of mouth advertising to family and friends of how wonderful the promotion was and how great the prize or prizes are is one of the best forms of advertising they could receive.

What Laws Govern Sweepstakes?

In the United States, sweepstakes regulation is both a federal and state matter. At the federal level, a few of the agencies that may have interest in sweepstakes promotions include: the Federal Trade Commission "FTC", the Federal Communications Commission "FCC", the United States Postal Service "USPS", and the United States Department of Justice "DOJ". At the state level, typically the State Attorney General's office is the place where consumer complaints are fielded that might yield results. Each state deals with the regulation of sweepstakes in their own unique manner. Some states like New York for instance require that any consumer sweepstakes that has a prize value of $5,000 or more must register their promotion within 30 days in advance of the beginning of the promotion. Another requirement is that the organization conducting the sweepstakes must post a bond for the value of the prizes. Florida requires a seven day advanced registration notice and has bonding requirements. In Rhode Island retail outlets offering sweepstakes with a prize valued more than $500 are required to register their promotion with the state.

With all the various rules and regulations, it is important for individuals themselves who take this hobby, passion or obsession seriously to familiarize themselves with the current laws both at the federal and state levels.

Practically speaking, the fervor and voracity to which sweepstakes laws are enforced is largely determined by the budget of each and every regulatory agency both at the federal and state level. The size and scope of the promotion itself plays a large role in the scrutiny it may receive. Simply put, in most cases, nationwide promotions will gain much more attention and focus than a small locally run promotion.

Federal and State Laws on Sweepstakes and Contests

The following information in this section was provided by the MPA - The Association of Magazine Media: http://www.magazine. org/sites/default/files/CONSUMER-Sweeps.doc

"The Association of Magazine Media is the primary advocate and voice for the magazine media industry, driving thought leadership and game-changing strategies to promote the medium's vitality, increase revenues and grow market share. Established in 1919, MPA represents 265 domestic, associate and international members. MPA is headquartered in New York City, with a government affairs office in Washington, DC."

Overview

Federal law governing the use of sweepstakes became effective in 2000. The federal law requires certain disclosures for mailed sweepstakes and prohibits certain practices. It also includes rules for skill contests.

Several states also have laws affecting sweepstakes and contests, some more restrictive than the federal law. In addition, given the global nature of the Internet, publishers involved with online sweepstakes should also be aware that laws in foreign nations may apply.

Federal Law

The federal law is the Deceptive Mail Prevention and Enforcement Act (DMPE), known commonly as the federal "Sweepstakes Law." The law applies only to material sent through the mail, and gives the U.S. Postal Service authority over and imposes affirmative disclosure and name removal requirements on sweepstakes and skill contest mailings. The Act also contains requirements for mailings containing facsimile checks, and mailings made to look like government documents.

When the Law Applies to Magazine Content

When Congress passed the DMPE, it included a significant exemption for magazine content, including advertising. The provisions of the law do not apply to sweepstakes and contests appearing in magazines if:

1. they are not directed at a named individual; or
2. they do not include the opportunity to make a payment or order a product or service.

General Provisions

As noted above, DMPE covers only sweepstakes promotions sent through the mail. It does not supersede state laws on sweepstakes. Thus, sweepstakes sponsors should review state requirements as well. Mailings that merely provide promotional information about a sweepstakes do not trigger application of the law—the sweepstakes promotion must include an opportunity to enter for the law to apply. All sweepstakes disclosures mandated by the law must be made in a "clear and conspicuous" manner that is "readily noticeable, readable, and understandable" to recipients.

Required Disclosures

Any solicitation to enter a sweepstakes or contest must contain the following information:

1. the official rules;
2. all terms and conditions for participating in the sweepstakes or contest;
3. the entry process;
4. the name of the sponsor or mailer of the sweepstakes;
5. the contact information for the sponsor or mailer of the sweepstakes

The official rules must include:

1. the estimated numerical odds of winning;
2. the number of prizes to be awarded;
3. the estimated retail value of the prizes to be awarded;
4. the nature of the prizes to be awarded; and
5. the schedule of payments if the prize is paid over time.

Sweepstakes solicitation mailings must include statements that no purchase is necessary to win and statements that purchasing the sponsors' products will not increase one's chances of winning. These statements must meet the following requirements:

1. they must be more conspicuous than the other required disclosures; and
2. they must appear in the following three places in a mailing:
   a. in the solicitation letter;
   b. in the order or entry form; and
   c. in the official rules

Required Disclosures for Skill Contests

Skill contests are defined by the Federal Trade Commission (FTC) as, "Puzzles, games or other contests in which prizes are awarded based on skill, knowledge or talent – not on chance." In these skill contests, sponsors must disclose:

1. the estimated number or percentage of participants who will win the skill contest;
2. the approximate number or percentage of participants who have won the sponsor's past three skill contests;
3. the judging methods;
4. the identity or a description of the qualifications of the judges;
5. the date on which winners will be selected;
6. the date or process by which prizes will be awarded;
7. the number of rounds of competition;
8. whether subsequent rounds of competition will be more difficult than early rounds; and
9. the maximum cost to enter the entire competition.

Prohibited Practices

1. Mailings must not indicate that those who do not purchase sponsors' products or services will not receive future sweepstakes mailings;
2. Mailings must not indicate that an individual is a winner unless that person has actually won;
3. Mailings cannot require that sweepstakes entries be accompanied by orders or payments for previously ordered products or services;
4. Mailings cannot contain inconsistencies within the official rules or disclosures.

Facsimile Checks

Facsimile checks must contain a disclosure on the face of the document indicating that the check is non-negotiable and that it has no cash value.

Opt-Out Requirement

Mailings for sweepstakes and contests must display clearly and conspicuously a toll free telephone number or address by which recipients can contact the sponsor to be removed from any future mailings.

Upon receipt of a removal request, the sponsor must remove the requester's name and address from mailing lists within 60 days.

Penalties for Non-Compliance

The Postal Service can assess penalties for violations of up to $1 million. The fines are $25,000 for mailings of fewer than 50,000 pieces, $50,000 for mailings of between 50,000 to 100,000 pieces, and an additional $5,000 for each 10,000 pieces above 100,000 up to a maximum fine of $1 million.

For violations of the opt-out provisions, recipients may sue for injunctive relief and damages up to $500 per violation which can be tripled for willful violations. In addition, mailers who mail solicitations "recklessly" to those requesting removal can face statutory penalties to the federal government of $10,000 per mailing, and penalties of up to $2 million for selling the names and addresses of individuals requesting removal from mailing lists.

State Laws

State prize and gift notification laws also regulate the offering of sweepstakes, gifts, prizes, and premiums. Such regulation may include specific disclosure requirements for sweepstakes and contests, prohibitions on conditioning the receipt of prizes or gifts on the purchase of a product, prohibitions on "everybody wins" sweepstakes and restrictions on the use of simulated checks. Many of these state laws also impose various disclosure requirements on the offering of gifts or premiums.

Alabama: Sweepstakes Solicitations – Ala. Code §§ 8-19D-1 to 8-19D-1 (2006).

Arkansas: Prize Promotion Act – Ark. Code. Ann. §4-102-101 to 4-102-109 (2006).

California: Prize Notification – Cal. Bus. & Prof. Code § 17537 (2006); Solicitation materials containing sweepstakes entries - Cal. Bus. & Prof. Code § 17539.15 (2006); Unlawful advertising; conditional offer of prizes or gifts – Cal. Bus. & Prof. Code §§ 17537 – 17537.1 (2006).

Colorado: Sweepstakes and Contests – Colo. Rev. Stat. §§ 6-1-802 to 6-1-804 (2006).

Connecticut: Sweepstakes – Conn. Gen. Stat. §§ 42-295 to 42-300 (2006).

Florida: Game Promotion Registration Law – Fla. Stat. Ann. § 849.094 (2006).

Georgia: Fair Business Practices Act – Ga. Code Ann. §§ 10-1-392 to 10-1-393 (2006).

Hawaii: Offers of gifts or prizes; unlawful – Haw. Rev. Stat. § 481B-1.6 (2006).

Illinois: Prizes and Gifts Act – Ill. Comp. Stat. Ch. 815 §§ 525/1 – 525/35 (2006); Offers of free prizes, gifts or gratuities; disclosure of conditions – Ill. Comp. Stat. Ch. 815 § 505/2P (2006).

Indiana: Promotional Gifts and Contests – Ind. Code Ann. §§ 24-8-1-1 to 24-8-6-3 (2006).

Iowa: Prize Promotions – Iowa Code §§ 714B.1 – 714B.10 (2006).

Kansas: Prize Notification – Kan. Stat. Ann. § 50-692 (2006).

Kentucky: Use of mailed document purporting to inform of winning a prize – Ky. Rev. Stat. Ann. § 365.055 (2006).

Louisiana: Promotional Contests – La. Rev. Stat. Ann. §§ 51:1721 – 51:1725 (2006).

Maryland: Offers of conditional prizes; exceptions – Md. Code Ann. Com. Law I § 13-305 (2006).

Michigan: Lotteries – Mich. Comp. Laws § 750.372a (2006).

Minnesota: Prize notices and solicitations – Minn. Stat. § 325F.755 (2006).

Nevada: Sales Promotions – Nev. Rev. Stat. §§ 598.131 – 598.139 (2006).

New Hampshire: Prizes and Gift Act – N.H. Rev. Stat. Ann. §§ 358-O:1 to 358-O:10 (2006).

New Jersey: Notification to person that he has won prize and requiring him to perform act – N.J. Stat. Ann. § 56:8-2.3 (2006).

New Mexico: Game Promotion Regulations – N.M. Admin. Code tit. 1 §§ 2.2.7 – 2.2.13 (2006).

New York: Game Registration Law – N.Y. Gen. Bus. Law § 369-e (2006); Prize Award Schemes – N.Y. Gen. Bus. Law § 369-ee (2006).

North Carolina: Prize Presentation Law – N.C. Gen. Stat. §§ 75-32 to 75-34 (2006).

North Dakota: Contest Prize Notices – N.D. Cent. Code §§ 53-11-01 to 53-11-05 (2006).

Ohio: Prizes – Ohio Admin Code § 109:4-3-06 (2006).

Oklahoma: Consumers Disclosure of Prizes and Gifts Act – Okla. Stat. tit 21 §§ 996.1 – 996.3 (2006).

Oregon: Contest, Sweepstakes and Prize Notification Rules – Or. Admin. R. §§ 137-020-0410 to 137-020-0460 (2006).

Rhode Island: Prizes and Gifts Act – R.I. Gen. Laws §§ 42-61.1-1 to 42-61.1-9 (2006); Games of Chance Registration Act – R.I. Gen. Laws §§ 11-50-1 to 11-50-8 (2006).

South Carolina: Prize and Gift – S.C. Code Ann. §§ 37-15-20 to 37-15-100 (2006).

South Dakota: Sweepstakes Prizes – S.D. Codified Laws §§ 37-32-1 to 37-32-18 (2006).

Tennessee: Promotions or inducements to sell goods, services or other products – Tenn. Code Ann. § 47-18-120 (2006); Prizes – Tenn. Code Ann. § 47-18-124 (2006).

Texas: Contests and Gift Giveaways – Tex. Bus. & Com. Code Ann. §§ 40.001 – 40.005 (2006).

Utah: Prize Notices Regulation Act – Utah Code Ann. §§ 13-28-1 to 13-28-9 (2006).

Vermont: Contests and Sweepstakes – Vt. Stat. Ann. tit. 13 § 2143b (2006).

Virginia: Prizes and Gifts Act – Va. Code Ann. §§ 59.1-415 to 59.1-423 (2006).

Washington: Promotional Advertising of Prizes – Wash. Rev. Code §§ 19.170.010 to 19.170.900 (2006).

West Virginia: Prizes and Gifts Act – W. Va. Code §§ 46A-6D-1 to 46A-6D-10 (2006).

Wisconsin: Prize Notices – Wis. Stat. § 100.171 (2006).

Wyoming: Promotional Advertising of Prizes – Wyo. Stat. Ann. §§ 40-12-201 to 40-12-209 (2006).

Contests

Many people use the words contest and sweepstakes thinking they are the same but they are not. The difference between a sweepstakes and a contest is that in a sweepstakes the element of winning is random and in a contest winning is based on the skill level displayed which is determined by specific criteria outlined by the official rules.

One common example would be that of a photo contest. In this type of a contest judges will likely assign point values to various criteria they expect all entrants to meet. Examples could include but are not limited to making sure the photographic entry carries the appropriate theme of the contest, shows originality, is creative, delivers the right message, is entertaining, is visually appealing and of course the color, exposure and lighting all have to be acceptable. Further, brands are often looking for a commercial appeal, and something that creates an impact. Again, the key to any contest is to read and re-read the rules carefully and make sure you are in fact meeting all the requirements.

The following is a list of the top mistakes made by people entering contests:

People show or mention material that is copyrighted. An example includes making a video or taking a picture of yourself wearing a hat showing the Under Armor® logo. No matter how good this submission might be it will likely be disqualified.

You will need to denote the name of a specific artist or band if you use a recording artist's music in a video. Be careful to not violate any trademark guidelines.

All submittals need to not include any profanity or nudity whatsoever, period.

Entries need to follow all the limitations exactly as described. This includes when submitting online paying close attention to the file size and any word counts.

Judges want to see originality and feel positive about what they viewed or read.

Once again the mistake is simply a failure to follow the rules.

Note that creating a contest seems fairly simple because almost anything that requires you to demonstrate a level of skill can be made into a contest. However, the tricky part comes in the actual judging aspect to make sure entrants are all treated fairly; this is another reason why people should contract with a professional judging agency for guidance.

The most common contests you will see advertised will be recipe, cooking, writing, video and photography. You will also see contests for art, drawing, design, music, poetry, speaking, songwriting and much more. There are also other more obscure contests like the NSS and NASA Ames Space Settlement Contest. See the following website for details: http://www.nss.org/settlement/nasa/Contest

Contests are supposed to be fun and exciting; unfortunately, some have turned deadly. Specifically, eating contests. It might surprise you, but every year several people die from choking in eating contest. Years ago a woman in California also died after drinking an excessive amount of water in a promotion dubbed "Hold Your Wee for a Wii." Sponsoring companies need to use common sense when developing any contest and understand that any activity that might be deemed risky should be avoided. Likewise, no contest should ever allow an intoxicated person to participate. At the very least the use of a disclaimer and waiver statement in the official rules is a must that states that the contestants acknowledge and expressly assume all risks for their actions.

BEFORE You Enter

Unfortunately, a lot of people who enter sweepstakes don't take the time to stop and study the rules of the sweepstakes they are about to enter. This is a very common mistake that often leads to time and money being wasted as well as being disqualified from the sweepstakes.

The official rules often appear to be written in legal jargon. But basically, these rules always mean what they say, so it's very important that you understand them. The sponsors of sweepstakes and contests are all required to create an official set of rules. These rules should be easily accessible and/or prominently displayed.

If you find a sweepstakes promotion that does not have any rules, then it is highly recommended that you avoid entering altogether!

Rules are in fact a contract between you the consumer and the sponsor of the sweepstakes. The official rules should contain information that clearly states that no purchase is necessary. Instructions should be clear as to how one could use an alternative method of entry in order to participate in the promotion. The contact information of the sponsor and the promoter of the sweepstakes should be prominently displayed.

Official rules once set in place and posted online should in no way be changed unless the change is minor, such as to correct a spelling error. If you notice rules changing midway through the sweepstakes then you should complain directly to the sponsor or judging agency and notify the Federal Trade Commission or your state attorney general office.

The official rules should clearly state the number of prizes, the retail values, and a statement of the odds. This statement is sometimes generic simply stating that in effect the odds are determined based on the total number of entries received.

All sweepstakes should list the beginning and end dates of the promotion and any individual and/ or geographic restrictions i.e. the sweepstakes is only open to those living in Texas or you must be 21 years of age or older in order to qualify.

In most cases the person entering the sweepstakes, at the very minimum, is required to provide his/her name and address. Many times an email or phone number is requested.

It is worth noting that many people subscribe to multiple sweepstakes newsletters or gather information online from various websites to find sweepstakes to enter. There is nothing wrong with using these tools of the trade, but you should still double check the information listed in the official set of rules.

One key element that separates the novice from the avid sweeper who enters sweepstakes is learning to be selective in what you enter. This may sound overly simple, but none of us have more than 24 hours to our day. So, we all need to make sure we are not wasting time on entering a sweepstakes for a prize we do not need or want. The novice may enjoy winning a prize for the sake of winning but the avid sweeper understands that time is valuable and it is best to focus all your attention on the prizes you really do want to win versus those that have little or no value to you.

Understanding Your Odds of Winning

Figuring the odds of winning a sweepstakes in process is nearly impossible because of so many different variables that go into each and every sweepstakes. All these different factors affect the odds and your ability to win. In almost every sweepstakes you will see this phrase or something similar in the official rules: "Odds of winning a prize depend on number of eligible entries received." No one except the sweepstakes sponsor and/or judging agency will know how many entries are actually received so trying to figure the odds in advance is impossible.

One small way to improve your odds of winning is to find sweepstakes that offer fewer ways a person can enter. Also, look for sweepstakes that have certain restrictions, such as age, gender or more commonly those restricting certain states from entering. The more restrictions the greater your odds.

All sweepstakes have specific rules as to the number of entries you are allowed to enter. Common sense would tell you that the more entries you send the better your odds, however, note that in sweepstakes like the HGTV® Dream Home where millions of entries are received sending in 100 entries versus 10 is going to greatly increase your statistical chance of winning; but in a sweepstakes with that number of entries, your chance to win is still a long shot. It is important to understand statistical difference vs. actual opportunity to win. Several years ago a mail order seller sold a booklet for $4.95 with the "secret of how a few dollars (fewer than $5.00) you could more than double your chance of winning your state lottery." He promised to give you double your money back if his system was not mathematically correct. The booklet was a bunch of lottery instructions but his "secret" was to buy a second ticket. If you had two tickets instead of one your chance of winning had just doubled! And if you bought three tickets your odds were way up.

Generally, the longer it takes a person to enter a sweepstakes the fewer people will enter. Sweepstakes that require a survey or those that want the entrant to perform extra tasks like taking and upload a photograph will also have fewer entries. The person's odds of winning will be affected by the prizes offered. The more prizes offered the more people enter to win those prizes. However, if the prize is a 10-foot-long, 400-pound, $7,000 Long Arm quilting machine, then one might assume fewer people will be interested. However, if a sweepstakes is well advertised, regardless of the prize, it will garner some number of entries. Look for sweeps that have limited advertising exposure.

Of course, your chance to win is also affected by the number of prizes. Of course, the fact that there are 10,000 winners of a potato cookbook may not be of interest. However, your chance to win in a sweepstakes with 10,000 prizes is usually significant.

Lastly, look for sweepstakes that offer shorter entry time periods. Next, enter as many times as allowable by the rules. Finally, don't forget to look for local sweepstakes where fewer entries are likely. Make sure to maximize the number of entries according to the rules and look to see if the sponsor allows for extra chances to win with a referral bonus entry.

Spotting Scams

By nature most people are excited when they get a letter, email or phone call notifying them that they are a winner of a prize. However, it never hurts to be skeptical and cautious. If you don't remember entering this specific sweepstakes then take your time and do your own investigation. Go online to make sure the sweepstakes is legitimate by looking for the sweepstakes itself and for a copy of the official rules.

As much as we might dream of large checks for thousands of dollars magically appearing in our mailbox overnight, it is best to focus on reality and stay in the moment. If you do get a random check- no matter how big or small the amount, **do not cash it**. Counterfeit checks and even counterfeit postal money orders exist and on some occasions cashing a check might actually be signing you up for a service or subscription you do not want. This deceptive advertising technique is accomplished by putting wording over the endorsement section. That is, the place where you endorse your $10.00 check might read "by depositing this check and endorsing below, you agree to a five year subscription to Recipe News Magazine." If you want to educate yourself about fake checks and lottery scams, the website http://www.fakechecks. org/ is an excellent online resource to review.

Any check that is as part of a promotion, must by law have a disclosure on the face of the document stating that the check is non-negotiable and has no cash value.

Be careful if the notification you received does not address you by name. When you receive a letter, check to see how it was mailed. If your letter was mailed bulk rate declaring you to be a winner, then realize many individuals are receiving the same notice.

A request that you send money to obtain your prize is a big red flag alerting you that this might be a scam. In a legitimate prize promotion, a winner never has to pay anything unless it is clearly stated in the rules. Some promotions offering a cruise as a prize might require the winner to pay port fees, gratuities or other incidental costs. If you receive a prize from overseas you might be required to pay any customs charges. In general, however, prize winners are rarely asked to pay fees before a prize can be awarded.

There are all types of money upfront scams, however, they usually take one of two forms.

FORM A: The letter arrives stating …"Congratulations you are the grand prize winner of $25,000." Elsewhere in the letter you are advised to send a check for $2.750 covering the federal sweepstakes tax; there is no such tax.

FORM B: The letter arrives stating … "Congratulations you are the grand prize winner of a sailboat (and/or computer, piano or anything else that needs to be shipped)." Elsewhere in the letter you are advised to send a check for $350 covering the freight charges. Remember, no legitimate sweepstakes ever charges the winner a delivery fee or any other fee.

Obviously, there are many variations of the above examples. Often times in the notification you get by mail there is a request asking for a bank certification fee, whatever that is, a vacation booking fee, an auto registration, license plate and state sales tax fee or even a small airline fee to cover the cost of issuing plane tickets or vacation vouchers. Again you need to be very careful and look at the official rules before paying anything upfront. Taxes, if any, are due later. Many times people have said, "Surely everyone knows this." Obviously not because these sweeps scams go on bilking many American consumers.

If taxes are due you will be instructed to pay any taxes directly to the Internal Revenue Service when you file your regular tax return.

Never wire money via Western Union™ or send money via a preloaded debit or credit card in order to claim a prize. No legitimate sweepstakes will ever ask you to wire money to "insure" delivery of any prize. Also, do not give your credit card number, pin code or security code to anyone in order to "win a prize." Do not give out any bank information, period! Any prize money you are entitled to receive will not be directly deposited into your bank account but will be sent to you via a check or gift card.

While enjoying a vacation on a cruise ship sounds like fun, be cautious if you receive an email or a letter that in part reads: "You have won a Free Cruise!" There are multiple "free cruise" offers and out right scams that are far from being actual cruises that are free. A few that occur frequently including receiving by mail an official looking letter that uses the logo of a prominent cruise line such as Carnival™ or Norwegian Cruise Line™. However, examining the letter closely, you will actually see that it is from a travel agent versus an actual cruise line who makes a large booking fee by signing you up for a cruise. So your free cruise voucher is not free after all. While this might not be a total scam, it is not a real free cruise either.

People have also reported getting a call notifying them that they won a free cruise and later are asked to provide a credit card number to hold their "free" cruise ticket. This, of course, is a scam.

While now defunct probably one of the most egregious peddlers of the "free cruise" deal was marketed under the name of Caribbean Cruise Line™. First off, Caribbean Cruise Line™ was not a cruise line at all, but the name of a wholesaler that offered these so called free cruises.

The fabulous cruise it turns out was not a seven night cruise or even a five night it was for two nights. Of course you can forget about Disney™, Holland American™ or NCL™ … it was a cruise on Caribbean Cruise Line™. Okay, you might be saying to yourself what's wrong with a free two night cruise? Well…first it was not really free, because you had to pay for government taxes and fees which may or may not have been disclosed until you made the final reservation. Next, you were pressured into considering a cabin upgrade then told about the added per day fee for gratuities and fuel surcharge. Of course, this did NOT include travel to the cruise ship which originally left from Palm Beach, Florida. Finally, after you had paid to get yourself (and your guest) to Florida you were told to go to the Fort Lauderdale "Welcome Center" to pick up your travel vouchers prior to boarding in Palm Beach. Yes, you pay for the $100 taxi ride from Ft. Lauderdale to Palm Beach.

Finally, when you boarded the ship you did not see a luxury cruise liner, you saw the Motel 6™ of cruise ships. The ships used for these cruises were converted ferries put out of service. In fairness, they did meet the U.S. and Caribbean coast guard standard safety regulations, but these cruises did not offer all the activities traditional cruise lines provide. Most of the available activities consisted of attending timeshare presentations or watching old movies.

With the advent of Facebook™ another variation has surfaced with pages that are created by scammer pretending to represent official cruise companies like Disney™ or Royal Caribbean™. The pages claim that you have the opportunity to win a free cruise by simply sharing a post. Unfortunately, there are no free cruises ever given away. Instead, the scammers are trying to build a large Facebook™ page following so they can then in turn push their products or services they want to sell in your newsfeed.

A quick tip that might be helpful when you surf Facebook™ is looking on the profile to see if it has either a blue badge checkmark or a grey badge checkmark. Both of these marks occur if Facebook™ has verified the page you are viewing as authentic.

So what else can you do to protect yourself? How do you make sure your cruise prize is a real prize? It's as easy as A-B-C.

A. If you won a cruise find out the name of the cruise line. If it's not NCL™, Disney™ or one of the major cruise lines it's probably "the good ship SCAM."

B. Find out who is running the sweepstakes. If it's not a major company or you did not actually enter their sweepstakes, you did not win a prize.

C. As soon as anybody asks you for any money. Be it $59 or $5.90 just know it's a likely scam!

Legitimate sweepstakes will often require winners to fill out an affidavit which is considered a legal document. Some may also make you have this document notarized which gives assurance to the sponsor that you are indeed who you claim to be to make sure the prize they are awarding goes to the right individual. Affidavits are almost always required when the value of the prize or prizes offered is more than $600. This dollar amount is the legal threshold whereby companies are required by law to generate a 1099-M Form that will be sent to you at the end of the year for you to file with your annual federal tax return. You can learn more about this in the section titled: What to do about taxes.

If you get notified by email that you have won a prize, pay close attention to the email address used. If it comes from a free email account like Hotmail™, Gmail™, Yahoo™ or any other than a company domain name then you need to be careful. Sometimes email addresses do look real at first glance because the company name might be included as part of the email but the last part of domain name may be different. Also, if you see words spelled incorrectly, pictures or logos in the email itself are not loading correctly, be cautious.

When you first receive notification think back carefully and try to remember if you even entered the particular sweepstakes in question. For avid sweepers this might be a challenge but remember, it is impossible to win a "lottery" if you never purchased a ticket! In short you need to beware of all notifications that you won anything especially if the notification is from a foreign lottery office or supposed government agency that might sound official such as the National Sweepstakes Bureau which does not exist. Legitimate sponsors may send out a winning notification by first class mail or opt to use an alternative carrier like FedEx™, UPS™, or DHL™.

Fake notifications can occur over the phone or via regular mail, email and even text messaging. If you receive a spam text message saying you won a gift card or some other prize, beware.

Many times these messages will seek to obtain additional personal information about you as well as get you to agree to sign up for "trial offers" that in many cases lead to monthly recurring charges.

You should avoid clicking any links sent to you when you do not personally know the individual or group that sent the message. Unfortunately, many times these hyperlinks you click will automatically install malware on your computer that will compromise your privacy.

Again, if you are unsure that you entered the sweepstakes or you feel something just does not look right then it would behoove you to do your own investigation online looking for the sweepstakes name, sponsor's name and the official rules. Remember that all legitimate sweepstakes will have a link to their official rules. These tips will help you in verifying your winning notification. Now is not the time to be shy or timid, instead directly contact the company or judging agency via email or by phone. Don't automatically reply to the email or use any phone number they may list in the email but instead look up the information for yourself online.

Beware of any email that appears to be pushy and requests that you act fast! The reason for the rush is that the scammer wants you to be careless and not think about the information he/she is asking you to disclose. Note that there are some legitimate judging agencies that do send out emails notifying winners and expect you to respond within 24 or 48 hours or you will forfeit your prize. This is the case when the prize might be more time sensitive like near an event date, or it may just be an internal policy because the agency is processing a lot of prize applications.

Millions of emails are sent out daily known as "phishing scams" where criminals are using the internet in hopes of getting unsuspecting people to give out more important information like social security numbers or bank account numbers so fraud can be committed. If you feel that you have been defrauded when using the internet you can file a complaint with The Federal Bureau of Investigation's Internet Crime Complaint Center known by the acronym IC3:

"The mission of the Internet Crime Complaint Center is to provide the public with a reliable and convenient reporting mechanism to submit information to the Federal Bureau of Investigation concerning suspected Internet-facilitated criminal activity and to develop effective alliances with law enforcement and industry partners. Information is analyzed and disseminated for investigative and intelligence purposes to law enforcement and for public awareness."

Source: http://www.ic3.gov/default.aspx

Lastly, when entering sweepstakes online if you see as part of the registration a CAPTCHA (Completely Automated Public Turing Test to Tell Computers and Humans Apart) test then in most cases this sweepstakes is legitimate.

Identity Theft Concerns

Many people who enter sweepstakes have real fear and concern about identity theft so it is important to know the facts and not base your decisions off ads you may have seen on TV that unfortunately are almost always geared towards promoting fear.

The honest truth of the matter is that identity theft is not something that can be 100 percent preventable. There is no magic button, no special product or service that you can buy to prevent this from occurring to you. Why, you might wonder. Well, the reason is simple. Think of all the financial transactions you make on a daily, weekly or even monthly basis. Supermarkets, gas stations, doctor visits, credit card companies, insurance companies and the list goes on and on. With each one of these transactions you are likely disclosing a certain amount of personal information and trusting that each and every transaction is 100 percent secure. We all know this is never going to be the case.

Resolving Identity Theft

Now let's review the actual reported facts by looking at a summary of the latest statistics reported by the Bureau of Justice Statistics. This facts sheet was obtained online from the following website: http://www.bjs.gov/content/pub/pdf/vit14_sum.pdf

Below are highlights from the report:

"An estimated 17.6 million Americans—about 7 percent of U.S. residents age 16 or older—were victims of identity theft in 2014. Most victims (86 percent) experienced the misuse of an existing credit card or bank account. About 4 percent of victims had their personal information activity stolen and used to open a new account or for other fraudulent activity. Some victims (7 percent) experienced multiple types of identity theft during the most recent incident. These findings were similar to those published in 2012."

"Resolving identity theft problems more than half (52 percent) of identity theft victims were able to resolve any problems associated with the incident in a day or less, while about 9 percent spent more than a month. Victims whose existing account was misused (54 percent) were more likely to resolve any financial or credit problems within 24 hours than victims of multiple types of identity theft (39 percent) or victims of new account fraud (36 percent)."

In conclusion while identity theft is a problem it is not one that should stop you from entering sweepstakes. While it has been said over and over read the rules of the sweepstakes before you enter. If you feel the least bit uncomfortable or don't see an address listed of the sponsor on the website then skip entering this sweepstakes and move on.

Need Help?

If you experience a problem with a sweepstakes promotion whom should you contact? You should first try to make contact with the judging agency or the sponsor of the promotion. If you still feel they have not resolved the issue or you feel as if the promotion might be a scam then you might want to contact the State Consumer Protection Office or the state office for the Attorney General.

A quick way to locate who to contact is by going to this government website and use the drop down list by state: https://www.usa.gov/state-consumer

Another option is to contact the National Fraud Information Center 1-800-876-7060 or www.fraud.org.

Other agencies that may have interest include:

US Postal Inspection Service
Criminal Investigation Service Center
222 S Riverside Plaza Ste. 1250
Chicago, IL 60606-6100
Phone: 1-800-372-8347
http://postalinspectors.uspis.gov

The following link will direct you to a downloadable form you can use to report mail fraud: http://about.usps.com/forms/ps8165.pdf

Federal Trade Commission
600 Pennsylvania Ave NW
Washington, DC 20580-0001
Phone: 1-877-FTC-HELP
https://www.ftccomplaintassistant.gov/
Information#crnt&panel1-1

If you need to report possible violations in England, Wales and Northern Ireland go online to https://www.police.uk/.

Not Everyone Can Win

Some sweepstakes theoretically are not open to everybody. In the first place, you are usually not allowed to enter a sweepstakes if you are a relative of someone employed by the sponsor or of the judging organization. Some sweepstakes are only regional or in the case of sweepstakes offered on radio or on a local television station you are required to be within a certain viewing or listening area.

Certain sweepstakes are geared toward people who are most likely to use the product that the company is promoting. In direct mail sweepstakes, major companies only mail out entries to the people whom they believe are most likely to purchase their magazines, books, or other products. Of course, even if you have no interest in these products, you are entitled to enter if you receive a form in the mail if the rules states so. That is, you may receive a subscription offer from Car Magazine™ and the rules may state open only to licensed drivers over the age of 21. You may get the mailing, but if you don't have a license you can't win.

Today sweepstakes are advertised and promoted in many different ways. Corporate websites, Facebook™ pages or Twitter™ accounts will likely be utilized when advertising a sweepstakes promotion. Stickers on the product package or a completely different package design are also common. In short, sweepstakes today can be just about anywhere!

Once you've entered a sweepstakes, the mechanics are fairly simple. For you, there's nothing more to be done. You sit back and wait until the drawing date. But what about the judging organization?

You'll notice in the rules that most sweepstakes say "random drawings." This is the case because: hundreds of thousands of entries are received in most sweepstakes. It would be impossible to put all the entries into a large drum, and draw from it. Instead the judges hold a series of drawings in which random samples are selected from each mail sack received. Finally, there is a drawing conducted by a blindfolded person who picks the winners out of a large drum or bag.

Most large corporations who run sweepstakes promotions on a regular basis contract with a promotional management company may also act as their judging agency. It is the job of these companies to ensure that all federal, state and local regulations are complied with. They can and often do perform certain tasks to ensure absolute objectivity of the promotion as well as the actual prize drawing or drawings and sometimes the actual fulfillment and distribution of the prizes themselves.

Over the last decade, however, due to budget cutbacks the role and involvement of these agencies now tend to vary from sweepstakes to sweepstakes. As the market has gotten more competitive quite a few of the newer and smaller agencies offer very low entry fees allowing many more smaller companies and organizations to use sweepstakes as a means to attract new customers and/or readers to their website. The lower fees also mean the actual hands on agency involvement in the promotion itself is much less.

The agency may create the official set of rules but leave the actual drawing aspect to in house marketing professionals who work for the company. In many ways this defeats the whole original purpose of having an independent judging agency. Nevertheless, this is the reality of what has happened in the industry.

The Official Rules

Avid sweepers are going to be spending a lot of time reading the official rules. It will be helpful to understand the legal jargon and know a little background of why the rules are stated in a certain fashion.

In a sweepstakes, your chances of winning are the same whether you purchase the product or not. This is not necessarily true in the case of contests. In contests, the element of chance is eliminated which means that it is acceptable for the manufacturer to require that you buy their product. But in a sweepstakes, the manufacturer can't ask you to buy anything. Make sure you follow the rules carefully. If the rules state a plain 3"x 5" card then do not use a card with lines.

Unfortunately, consumers have been known to use the back of a sheet of paper which they've written their name and address, an old letterhead, old envelopes, or anything but the piece of paper required. This is not the time and place to save a couple of pennies. Make sure you use exactly what the rules call for and make sure you print.

In the not so distant past official rules would often use the phrase, "print in block letters," directing people how they wanted an entry to be presented. In the mind of the judge, block letters means non-cursive, printed letters.

The one key phrase in almost all sweepstakes promotions is the phrase, "No purchase necessary." This should be stated clearly and prominently. In fact, this is a requirement by law in many states, and you will typically see this at the beginning of the Official Rules and often in bold capital letters.

If you see the phrase, "Purchase will not increase your chance of winning," realize this phase is a requirement under the Federal Deceptive Mailing and Enforcement Act for direct mail promotions.

The phrase, "Open only to legal residents of the 50 United States and D.C." often is confusing to some who may misinterpret this clause thinking that the sweepstakes is open to ALL residents of the United States. This is not the case because this language excludes Puerto Rico, the Virgin Islands, America Samoa and Guam.

Many times you will see stated in online promotions, "Entrants must be 13 or older." This phrase is required by the Federal Children's Online Privacy Protection Act that deals with promotions that are directed towards children.

Some courts hold that sweepstakes' "Official Rules" are in fact a contract that is a binding agreement between both the individual entering the sweepstakes and the sponsor. This is why in some cases you will notice the rules stating that, "Entrants must be 18 or older." Eighteen is the age of consent whereby a person can enter into a binding contract. The noted exceptions to this age rule include Mississippi where you have to be 21 and in Alabama and Nebraska where the age of consent is 19.

In many sweepstakes you will see variations of the following wording: "Employees or sponsor and anyone associated with this promotion, as well as their family and household members are not eligible." The obvious reason for including this language in any sweepstakes is to show the seriousness the sponsor has made to ensure that there is no impropriety or even the appearance of such in the administration of how the promotion is conducted or how the potential winners are selected.

The language, "Approximate retail value (ARV) of the sweepstakes prize is X," is a requirement by law in certain states.

Many times people will read in the rules the phrase, "By participating, you grant the sponsor permission to use your name, photographic, voice, any other likeness, or comments for publicity purposes, in any and all media, now known or hereafter devised, without further compensation, unless prohibited by law." In the state of Tennessee, a law has been passed whereby the sponsor cannot require the individual winner to agree to a publicity release.

As mentioned before many states deem the "Official Rules" as a binding contract, regardless, in some states, namely Massachusetts, New York, Rhode Island, Vermont and Wisconsin, there is a requirement for a release to be written and signed by the releaser before a prize can be awarded. For this reason you will see listed in the rules: "Winners will be required to sign a prize release."

"IRS Form 1099 will be issued to the winner." Unfortunately, under IRS regulation when a prize is won with a value of $600 or more the sponsor is required by law to issue this form to the winner. This 1099-M Form should be filed with your taxes!

In many sweepstakes you will see, "If due to printing, production or other error, more prizes are claimed than are intended to be awarded for any prize level, the intended prizes will be awarded in a random drawing from among all verified and validated prize claims received for that prize level. In no event will more than the stated number of prizes be awarded."

This clause is often referred to in the sweepstakes business as the "Kraft Clause" due to a 1989 lawsuit that took place in their "Ready to Roll" promotion where printing errors caused 10,000 entrants to have valid claims. Oops!

Toward the end of most sweepstakes rules you will see: "All winners will be determined in random drawings conducted by an independent judging organization."

There are quite a few firms that specialize in the design and implementation of prize promotions. One of the services they will likely perform is the actual drawing of the entries. The technique used for drawing entries will vary by agency but as mentioned before most hold a series of drawings in which random samples are selected from each mail sack received.

Other rules you will often see include: "No substitutions are made in the awarding of prizes. Only one prize is allowed per family. Winning odds are determined by the number of entries received. All prizes will be given away."

These rules mean pretty much what they say. You must remember even if you win, you can't choose your prize. The prize is chosen for you. You'll know what the prizes are from the original sweepstakes ad.

One reason why you can't expect substitutions is that many companies receive the prizes free from other companies. This may not make much sense to you, but it's a good advertising ploy for a company to give away its products or services. In other cases, the prizes are purchased by the company in advance.

"No substitutions" means you get what you win, and you win what you get. So, if you don't want the prizes offered, enter another sweepstakes.

In some cases, only one prize is allowed per family. Many companies feel that it would not look right for the same family to win two or more prizes. To the casual onlooker, it looks like one family is winning everything or as though there is collusion of some sort. However, one prize per family is not always the rule. In some sweepstakes, one family is allowed more than one prize. This is most often true when the prizes are small.

The matter of odds is simple enough to understand. If 1,000,000 contestants enter the sweepstakes, your chances of winning will be fewer than if 1,000 contestants enter. In both cases the sweepstakes might be otherwise exactly the same, but the latter case, the judge has to select from only a few entries. Naturally, yours is more likely to be chosen.

"To obtain a list of the winners, send a SASE to…" Many people just assume this is the sponsor's way of being transparent. While this might be the case, it is also a requirement under the law in the states of Florida, Maryland, Maine, New York, Rhode Island, and Tennessee as well as in Michigan and Wisconsin when sweepstakes are in game packs.

What about all these rules? Well, it's extremely important that you follow all of them carefully. They are so simple! If you make a mistake, your entry, even if it's a winner, will be disqualified. When you're reading the rules, underline the important points that you'll need to remember. Use a pen or highlighter, and make sure that you underline the closing date. But remember, each rule is important, and in order to win, you must follow all the rules.

Qualifiers - Additional Things to Consider

When entering mail-in sweepstakes the following are essential points you need to pay very close attention to in order for your entry to be acceptable and not disqualified.

Print your name, address, zip code, email address and date of birth on a plain piece of paper. In most cases the paper or card size of 3" x 5" is stated. On some occasions the rules state the information required is to be placed on a postcard.

Plain 3" x 5" pads are available at almost all office supply stores. This, by the way, is the exact size of an index card. Although index cards tend to be more expensive than plain pads of paper, they are often more readily available. For this reason, the extra expense may be worth it. Note that if the official rules call for paper it is recommended that you use a piece of paper even though an index card is technically paper.

Oftentimes the official rules specifically state that you print your name and address. The reason for this is obvious. The judges have to read thousands of entries, and it's important for you as well as them to make their work as easy as possible. Writing in script or cursive letters will eliminate your chances of winning. Always try to print as legibly as possible.

Another thing to watch out for is the zip code requirement. Leaving out your zip code may make the difference between getting a prize and not getting a prize. Certain prizes are shipped by third-class mail and the post office requires zip codes on all third-class mail. The manufacturer, the independent judging organization, or whoever chooses the winning entries often will eliminate your entry because you did not follow the rules and include your zip code.

Don't assume that just because you have all the required information written on the right card or paper size that your entry will be qualified to win. If a specific order is asked for in the rules, i.e. name, date of birth, address and email address then that is exactly how they should be written!

The term "enter as often as you like," obviously means what it says, but the key is to mail each entry separately. Any independent judging organization can tell you about crate loads of entries which were received with separate entry blanks that were packaged together in one box or envelope. Obviously, these entries were not acceptable.

In almost all cases entries must be mailed separately. If you are sending in 10 entries, you must send each in a separate envelope. If you are sending in 10,000 entries, you must send in 10,000 separate envelopes. Each and every entry form or 3" x 5" card or paper or needs to be filled out correctly as required in the official rules.

The mail-receipt date is the date by which the entry must be received by the independent judging organization. Unfortunately, the postal service in this country has not always been known for its efficiency. This is not your fault, but the judging organization doesn't accept late entries. Your entry is either there, or it isn't. If it's not there, you can be sure you won't win any prizes.

Another word of caution. Neatness and consideration for the judges play a large part in qualifying your entry. Most judges are irritated by what may seem to you the most unlikely things. Avoid stapling your entry or using tape or anything else that may cause entries to stick together. If a judge has to take time to detach a mess, then they may automatically disqualify the entry and toss it out. Keep your papers clean. There's nothing less appealing to a tired judge than black ink smears and soiled paper.

Sweepstakes Exclusions

Oftentimes you will notice in the official rules that certain states are excluded from entering. Have you ever wondered why? If you happen to live in one of these states, this can really put a damper on your ability to enter and win. Below are just a few of the many different exclusionary rules and regulations sponsors are required to abide by when creating their sweepstakes promotion.

New York and Florida are two states that have a requirement for sponsors to register in advance of the promotion. In New York, the time is 30 days and in Florida advance registration is seven days. In New York if the prize value exceeds $5,000 a surety bond or a certificate of deposit is required that is equal to the total prize value. Florida also has another requirement whereby if the promotion is advertised in any print media such as a magazine with national circulation or direct mail sent to Florida residents, then a set of official rules must also be included. Radio and television ads are required to disclose that no purchase is necessary, explain any eligibility restrictions, as well as state the promotion end date and how one can go about obtaining a copy of the official rules.

Rhode Island requires an advanced registration fee of $150 to be paid to the secretary of state when the total value of all prizes exceeds $500 including if the sweepstakes is advertised in retail outlets.

The states of California, Tennessee and Utah have restrictions on sponsors that sell alcohol including the distribution of any alcohol related prizes.

Sweepstakes that are tobacco related are not allowed in Massachusetts, Michigan and Virginia.

In West Virginia sponsors of bottle cap promotions are required to provide retail outlets free bottle caps to distribute upon request.

Montana does not allow certain dairy promotions.

When entry forms are required the laws of Wisconsin require that retailers be allowed to request these forms on package promotions and do not allow milk to be used as a premium.

In Alabama in order to qualify for online prizes, you must be at least 19 years of age.

Beyond legal reasons you will find that some sponsors choose to exclude certain states or territories like Alaska, Hawaii, Puerto Rico, the Virgin Islands, America Samoa and Guam because sending prizes to those locations is cost prohibitive.

Not All Sweepstakes are Equal

It is a fact that not all sweepstakes are equal. The following is a case in point: "The Million Dollar Sweepstakes," was a promotion offered by Bauer Magazine L.P. Anyone who first glances at the title and begins to dream about winning a million dollars can't help but be enticed to jump at the opportunity. However, when you look closer you will find the odds of you actually winning are a lot slimmer than you might imagine.

Looking at the rules you will find that this promotion is actually listed on 12 different websites. Additionally, according to the rules you are allowed to enter one entry per person, per website URL, per day. So, each individual has the opportunity to enter 12 times per day. The stated promotion period for this sweepstakes was from January 16, 2015, and ended at 11:59 p.m. PT on December 31, 2015. The rules also stated the following:

"Grand Prize Drawing and Odds: On or about January 19, 2016, the Promotion Administrator will conduct a random drawing from among all eligible entries received during the entire Promotion Period from all URLs. One entrant (the "Finalist") will be selected. Odds of being selected as the Finalist will depend on the number of entries received. Finalist will then be entered into a Grand Prize event drawing, where Finalist will have a 1:250 chance of winning the Grand Prize. The process for random selection for the grand prize event drawing shall be determined solely by the Administrator. Further, the final date and location of the Grand Prize event drawing are subject to Sponsor's discretion. If Finalist does not win the Grand Prize, it will not be awarded, and Finalist Guaranteed Prize will be awarded."

"Prizes, Approximate Retail Value ("ARV") & Odds: One (1) Grand Prize: One million dollars ($1,000,000) to be paid as an annuity of $25,000 per year, for forty years, without interest (ARV based on present value: $515,000). Grand Prize will be awarded, only if the Finalist wins the Grand Prize Event Drawing, as described above. If Finalist does not win the Grand Prize, Finalist will instead receive the Finalist Guaranteed Prize of $5,000."

"Total ARV of all prizes, based on present value, is up to $515,000. Winner may be required to provide a photo for use by Sponsor. No substitution, cash redemption or transfer of prizes is permitted except at Sponsor's sole discretion or as provided herein. If a prize, or any portion thereof, cannot be awarded for any reason, Sponsor reserves the right to substitute a prize of equal or greater value. All federal, state and local taxes, and all other costs associated with acceptance or use of the prize(s), are the sole responsibility of the winner(s). Arrangements for delivery of prize(s) will be made after winner validation. Odds of winning a prize depend on the number of entries received. Odds of the Finalist winner receiving the million dollar prize is 1:250. By accepting the annuity, the Grand Prize winner agrees to release the Promotion Parties from all liability and responsibility for payments of the prize and acknowledges that such liability and responsibility shall rest only with the annuity company from which the annuity is purchased for the winner. At the Sponsor's discretion, unclaimed prizes may not be awarded."

Source: http://winit.intouchweekly.com/sweepstakes/one-million-dollar-giveaway-6423/rules

So, let's do a recap of what we've found. After reading the above information you see that the Grand Prize will be awarded, only if the Finalist wins the Grand Prize Event Drawing. If you lose, you get $5,000. Further the odds of the Finalist winner receiving the million dollar prize is 1:250. If you beat the odds and are fortunate to win then congratulations but realize it will take you 40 years to collect! Still with all this said, you do have a chance of winning a million dollars, but needless to say the odds are not in your favor!

Here is another example...

This online sweepstakes was found at: http://www.dealmaxx. net/p/cash1.html

The single webpage states: "What if...It only took minutes to get $10,000."

There is a space to enter your email and a button to click that says, "Start Winning Now." Below that you read: "Stop imagining and find out. Sign up for LAS's exclusive promotions and a chance to win $10,000."

It doesn't sound all that bad, does it? You might change your mind when you click the link to the rules: http://lsa.lifescript.com/advantage/lsaswpsrules.aspx/

It takes a moment, but eventually you get to the good part that reads:

"1. Prize. The prize for the Promotion is Ten Thousand and No/100 Dollars ($10,000.00), approximate retail value = $10,000.00 (the "Prize"). If there is a winner (see Section 7 below), only one (1) Prize will be awarded. THERE IS NO GUARANTEE THAT THE PRIZE WILL BE AWARDED. Taxes, fees or other charges, if any, are the sole responsibility of winner(s). By accepting the Prize, winner releases and discharges Sponsor Entities, information providers, content providers, advertisers, advertising agencies, promotional and marketing agencies, and any other companies involved with or otherwise providing services related to this Promotion, and all their respective employees, officers, directors, representatives and agents from any liability or damage due in whole or in part to the award, acceptance, possession, use or misuse of the Prize or from participation in this Promotion."

Bummer, so there is no guarantee that the prize will be awarded. But wait it gets better.

"1. Odds of Winning. The odds of winning the Prize are 25,000,000 -1. The total number of entries for the Promotion is limited to 25,000,000, and as such, the number of entries actually received will not impact the odds of winning.

2. Winner Selection. Prior to the start of the Promotion Period, the Administrator will randomly determine one (1) eight (8) digit prize determination number (the "Prize Determination Number") for the Sweepstakes, and provide the Prize Determination Number to the Sponsor in encrypted form. Until the encryption key is provided, the Prize Determination Number will be known only to the Administrator. Such Prize Determination Number shall be a whole number between 00,000,000 and 25,000,000. When an entrant enters the Sweepstakes by following the steps described in Rule 5 above, Sponsor will securely, electronically store that entry.

At the end of the Promotion Period, the Sponsor will bundle all entries in the Promotion, and using a random number generator, will randomly generate one (1) eight (8) digit number between 00,000,000 and 25,000,00 to be associated with each individual entry (the "Participant Number"). The list of each entry and the corresponding Participant Numbers will then be sent to the Administrator. At such time, the Administrator will provide Sponsor with the encryption key and Sponsor will compare the Prize Determination Number to the Participant Numbers. If the Prize Determination Number and the entrant's Participant Number match identically, the entrant will the winner of the Prize, subject to verification of eligibility and compliance with these Official Rules. If there is a winner, the winner will be notified by email and regular mail."

Wow, that sure was a mouth full wasn't it. The reason for this example is simply to point out that you must be very careful before you click your mouse to enter. It can't be stressed enough, READ THE RULES.

One final point, there does appear to be a rise in the number of sweepstakes that offer large prizes, such as cars, that require, people being credited with an entry if they purchase some promotional product like a tee shirt or hat as well as those who use an alternative means of entry. In many cases websites offering these type promotions will not provide much information about the sponsor company involved. In most instances, there does not appear to be any real judging agency involvement. All these are red flags and promotions like these, even if they are listed in a sweepstakes newsletter, should probably be avoided.

Finding and Entering Sweepstakes

Long before the internet people had to rely mainly on listening to the radio and reading the newspaper to find sweepstakes. Supermarkets were another avenue where sweepstakes promotions were often found along with official entry blank pads and boxes to place those entries. Today you no longer have to rely on just those methods of entry.

You will find a few places that may have an occasional entry box but the vast majority of sweepstakes you will find will be listed online. Yet it still does not hurt when making your weekly trip to the grocery store to go with a pad and pen in hand, or use your smart phone for the purpose of scouting for on package promotional sweepstakes giveaways. Scan your local and regional newspapers as well for new store openings and other special events which sometimes mean a chance for free prizes for those who show up.

Local and regional sweepstakes are often easier to win because fewer people will enter. In sweeping think local, regional, national then cyberspace!

The internet has opened up a whole new world of promotions. Individuals as well as large corporations all are keenly interested in selling their product and/or service to you, the consumer, and they are desperately trying to rise above the noise to get your attention. One way this is accomplished is by creating a promotion using the time-tested method of offering a sweepstakes.

In most cases, your name and email address are required at the minimum to enter. More information, like your address, is sometimes required as well as making you check a box that states that you agree to the official rules. Sometimes, sponsors will also ask you to check a box to receive additional communication via email but this should never be a requirement.

At any given moment, there are literally thousands of these types of sweepstakes promotions happening online daily. This means more entries are being accepted by promotions than ever before so the odds of winning vary depending on the rules listed in the promotion. The larger the number of entries the lower the odds of winning, especially if the promotion happens to allow unlimited entries versus only allowing one entry per person or per household.

The Good Old Entry Box

If you ever find yourself sliding your name into an entry box with hopes of being drawn for a prize, there are two possible secrets that may help you win more. While there has been no scientific study done to prove these methods are correct, it does make sense.

The first method was said to have been developed in late 1970s by Thomas Knight an advertising executive in New York who came up with the "Knight Fold" idea of simply folding the entry on the diagonal allowing the entry to form in a tent like fashion. Another method involves an "accordion fold" with hopes that the additional pleats will allow the entry to be grasped easier. Basically both seek to increase the "feel ability" of the entry by adding more dimension, altering the entry form allowing it to be chosen easier.

Tip: Beware, many times those entry boxes close to the door at restaurants or in supermarkets often touting a free prize weekend giveaway are nothing more than gimmicks used by high pressure time share sales people to gather names.

Also, sweepstakes sponsor should note that in some states like Ohio if it is determined that the primary reason the person visiting a location is to enter the sweepstakes then that action is deemed "consideration" which makes the promotion illegal.

Radio/Phone-In Sweeps

In order to take advantage of the different promotions that are taking place in your area you are going to need to listen to lots of different radio stations. You will quickly find a pattern in the times they announce the phone in contest. Using your flash and redial buttons will help in calling faster. You might want to consider using both your cell phone and home or office phone at the same time to increase your chances of winning. Obviously, having numbers on speed dial helps. Write down any information you need and keep it by your phone. Remember persistence pays off.

Entering Sweepstakes by Mail

Much like entering online, finding sweepstakes to enter by mail is not going to be a problem. A key to help improve your odds slightly is finding mail-in sweepstakes that do not have an online component. Generally, the fewer ways a person can enter the sweepstakes the better for those entering.

Everyone realizes that entering online is fairly quick and easy; the main cost is the individual's time. With mail-in sweepstakes the person's time is just one of the many cost components for entering a specific sweepstakes. Since you are spending your hard earned dollars before you place another stamp on an envelope, you need to really assess the value of the prizes offered and if the risk of mailing the entries is worth the potential reward.

You will find that the cost of the supplies quickly adds up. You will need pens, envelopes, papers and cards and, of course, postage.

Let's break each one of these down. First, let's talk about pens. For many this is a personal preference, but regardless you want a pen that offers a good quality ink that will not smear. A recommendation would be the Uni-Ball® 207™ Retractable Fraud Prevention Gel Pens. Notice that only using a pen was mentioned. When filling out a sweepstakes entry you should never use a pencil.

Next let's talk about envelopes. Many sweepstakes specify using a #10 envelope because this is the business standard size. Since many sweepstakes call for this envelope size it would be safe to say this is the standard. If you choose to use another size then that is your prerogative. However, if the rules state using a #10 envelope using any other would be foolhardy. Another thing you should consider when purchasing your envelopes is the type of closure of the envelope and the thickness of the envelope. The peel and stick version security envelope makes the process fast and simple plus the envelope thickness is adequate to prevent tearing.

Choosing paper and cards to be used for your sweepstakes entry forms is again a personal choice. Most people use unlined index cards versus lined cards.

Lastly, the all-important topic of postage. If you want to find a deal on postage the best place to look is on eBay™. Normally you can find many different auctions that sell postage less than face value. The best deals usually come from buying lots of lower denomination stamps that are the older gum label variety that may require you to use a glue stick.

However, if in reading the description you have any doubt that that stamps offered may have been used then you should NEVER attempt to re-use that stamp for any reason because it is illegal to do so and the penalties are severe if you are caught.

Title 18, U.S. Code, Sections 471 and 1720 states:

"Whoever, with intent to defraud, falsely makes, forges, counterfeits, or alters any obligation or other security of the United States, shall be fined under this title or imprisoned not more than 20 years, or both.

Whoever uses or attempts to use in payment of postage, any canceled postage stamp, whether the same has been used or not, or removes, attempts to remove, or assists in removing, the canceling or defacing marks from any postage stamp, or the superscription from any stamped envelope, or postal card, that has once been used in payment of postage, with the intent to use the same for a like purpose, or to sell or offer to sell the same, or knowingly possesses any such postage stamp, stamped envelope, or postal card, with intent to use the same or knowingly sells or offers to sell any such postage stamp, stamped envelope, or postal card, or uses or attempts to use the same in payment of postage; or

Whoever unlawfully and willfully removes from any mail matter any stamp attached thereto in payment of postage; or

Whoever knowingly uses in payment of postage, any postage stamp, postal card, or stamped envelope, issued in pursuance of law, which has already been used for a like purpose —

Shall be fined under this title or imprisoned not more than one year, or both; but if he is a person employed in the Postal Service, he shall be fined under this title or imprisoned not more than three years, or both."

It is worth noting that The United States Post Office sells both postcards and envelopes that already have the postage affixed that cost a few cents more than the regular postage cost.

Postcard Entries

If the official rules state that your entry should be by postcard, you can use either the standard pre-stamped postcards sold by the United States Post Office, or you can purchase or make postcards to send. However, before you get too crafty, it is important for you to be keenly aware of the United States Post Office regulations when it comes to postcards.

On the USPS website, they have a section titled: Business Mail 101. For your convenience we have copied the information below:

"You may think that your mail piece is a 'postcard,' because it is a single sheet of paper. But to qualify for mailing at the First-Class Mail postcard price, it must be:

- Rectangular
- At least 3 ½ inches high x 5 inches long x 0.007 inch thick
- No more than 4 ¼ inches high x 6 inches long x 0.016 inches thick

If your mail piece does not meet the dimensions above, then the Postal Service considers it a letter and letter-size postage is charged. With Standard Mail, there is a little more flexibility – there is no separate (lower) price for postcards, so you don't have to worry about your postcard being too big – because you're paying letter prices anyway. But make sure that your postcard is no larger than 6⅛" x 11½" x ¼" thick. Mail pieces larger than any of those dimensions and you'll have to pay flats (large envelope) postage prices."

"Some mailers want to attach stickers, magnets, or other items to their postcards. However, an attachment may disqualify the mail piece for mailing at the First-Class Mail postcard price—or even make it non-mailable."

Source: https://pe.usps.com/businessmail101

Many people have found that in order for postcard entries not to be returned by mistake, it is best to turn the postcard sideways when you fill out your name and address and any other required information. This insures that your information is not confused as the mailing address.

The postage for postcards should be affixed in the upper right hand corner. Directly below the stamp is the area for your mailing address. Note that you need to leave space at the bottom of the postcard, the maximum of 5/8 inch in width. This area is the location of the bar code that the post office will print on your postcard to route it to the proper address.

Finally, know that for whatever reason some sponsors and even some judging agencies handling sweepstakes mistakenly ask individuals to mail in a 3" X 5" postcard for your entry. Obviously, you know by reading the above that this size is too small and will be rejected by the postal systems so you have two choices to make. First you can either put your entry on a 3" X 5" card and mail it in a standard number #10 envelope or use either an official USPS postcard or another size that is acceptable and mail that instead.

Mail Delivery

Many sweepers who enjoy mail-in sweepstakes often ignore two critical elements: the postmark date and the actual expected delivery date. The time when first class mail being processed and delivered within a few days is long over.

In 2012 and 2013, 141 processing facilities were closed. In 2015 there were 320 processing plants that handled 142.2 billion pieces of mail. The United States Postal Service handles 47 percent of the world's mail volume.

The current USPS standard for the delivery of first-class mail within the continental United States is now three to five days. However, recent reports have shown that the actual delivery times for some mail is slower. Nationwide 63 percent of single-piece, first-class mail was delivered within the standard three-day delivery window, while the remaining 37 percent took longer.

Designer Envelopes

Many avid sweepers will swear that they feel their chances of winning are improved by having envelopes that are brightly colored or decorated. Regardless, the most important thing to remember is that you need to be very careful if you are adding attachments to either envelopes or postcards. You don't want to disqualify the mail piece for mailing at the First-Class Mail rate or worse make the item non-mailable.

Below is a small list of individuals that offer unique and creative envelopes that will surely jazz up your entries. To find out the latest designs and prices by contacting them now.

Sandy Coates
Email: sacoates1@msn.com
Jo's Hand Decorated Envelopes
Email: jbhotchkiss@att.net

Hand Printing Services

For those who love a good mail-in sweepstakes, there are times when filling out hundreds of papers, cards or postcards and envelopes can become a real chore and just impossible to complete on time. Fortunately there are quite a few individuals who are glad to help for a fee. Contact them for their current pricing, you will be surprised how reasonable their rates can be.

Jennifer Day Handprinting
    Jennifer Day
    Email: jennday3@icloud.com

Pat's Hand-Printing
    Pat Peckham
    Email: repat133@aol.com

Cortney's Handprinting
    Cortney Sneller
    Email: C_sneller@yahoo.com

Winning Requires That You Follow the Directions

Read the rules: The "official rules" for a sweepstakes can be difficult to find at times, but you need to know the rules of the game. Make the effort to read the rules to learn how many times you can enter and when you can enter. Also note if the sweepstakes is one per person or per household, daily, weekly, monthly or something different. Some sweepstakes are for only certain regions of the county so don't assume that all sweepstakes are open to everyone. Verify this information before you make the effort to enter.

Follow the rules: Nothing is more frustrating than entering a sweepstakes only to find out later that your entry or entries were disqualified because you did not follow the rules. Following the rules sounds so simple but judging agencies frequently report that a large number of all entries are discarded because entrants did not follow the rules.

Separate the tasks of entering the sweepstakes: Henry Ford taught us a long time ago that assembly line operations get more work done faster.

If you divide up the tasks of entering the sweepstakes, you'll find that you get more done in less time. Enlisting others to help can be a real bonus. Set up an assembly line production. Have one person fill out the entry form; have another person address the envelope and place the entry form inside, and finally have someone check to make sure the address is correct. Then seal the envelope and place the proper postage on the envelope.

Many people have a box or bin mailing system. Entries are tagged by date and stacked in order so only certain envelopes are mailed each day. Remember, the key to winning is entering often and paying close attention to both the beginning and ending dates of the promotion. If you do a lot of mail-in entries make sure you double check to see that postage is affixed.

Abbreviate as much as possible: Unless the rules state for you to use your full name only use your first and last name when entering to save time. Abbreviate your address when possible. Again, in this way you'll find that you can enter more often. Obviously, "NE" for Nebraska is going to take a lot less time than spelling out the state. As a word of caution, make sure it's a common abbreviation. If the judge can't understand what you've written, they will disqualify your entry. Don't ever invent abbreviations. If you have a question, look up words in the dictionary. It will take more time the first time and less time later on.

What goes inside: A 3" x 5" card or 3" x 5" paper perhaps? Wait, isn't a 3" x 5" card paper? Well, technically yes a 3" x 5" card is made of paper, but if the judging agency has made the distinction in the rules to specifically state you enter your information on a 3" x 5" piece of paper then you should always use a piece of 3" x 5" paper. If the rules ask you to put your entry on a 3" x 5" card then you should use a card. Note that while 3" x 5" is the most commonly required size other sizes may be required. Never assume you know what to use until you read the rules.

Now let's discuss what goes on the outside of your entry. A common mistake many people commit is not handwriting the envelope when the rules specifically call for envelopes to be hand written. Another rule breaker happens when the outer envelope is incorrectly addressed and not EXACTLY as the sponsor requests. In some cases there are multiple drawings taking place during the sweepstakes. Sponsors may ask that you include something in the lower left corner of the outer envelope to help distinguish the different drawing periods. Failing to do so gets your entry disqualified. Again as mentioned prior, be careful that you are not using the wrong size envelope when a #10 envelope is requested; breaking this rule will only get you disqualified.

Finally, one of the saddest ways entries fail is due to their lack of readability. You should never use a pencil unless it is called for but use ink instead. Also, if your handwriting is poor print your entry in block letters.

Decorate or Not Decorate: Every judging agency on the planet will tell you that when they conduct a drawing for a sweepstakes versus a contest where entries are judged that the drawing is done in a totally random manner. You will never see printed in any sweepstakes rules that colored envelopes or envelopes that are embellished with stickers or artwork have a better chance at winning than those that do not. But the question in many people's minds is will this help me win? Well, it might, but it may make it more difficult for the post office to process your entry without tearing as well. The decision is yours to make.

Weighted or Thicker Envelopes: A less commonly talked about tactic some sweepers use is having envelopes that are made of heavy stock paper or even inserting an extra piece of cardboard or other item in your entry to make it thicker in size. Depending on the weight and/or thickness extra postage may be due. Another possible downside can occur with your entry being torn while being processed at the post office. A judging agency could also disqualify you for adding additional material to your entry.

Entering family and friends: On the surface it might seem like a good idea to enter family and friends, but a problem can arise when they are notified of a win that they have no knowledge of entering or worse the email you use for them is one that they rarely check and end up losing out on winning a big prize. Also, if you are entering these entries using the same computer, then it will register the same IP address and those entries may be disqualified. One known example is the judging agency, ePrize™, has confirmed that they disqualify people who enter multiple names using the same IP address.

Check your email: Another real-life example occurred when on more than one occasion multiple email accounts were used for a spouse for online sweepstakes. The email account was not checked on a regular basis, and there was an email notifying the receiver of a win, but it required a response within 48 hours or the prizes would be fortified. Again, all the effort put into winning was smashed because of a failure to pay attention to the details. The lesson learned in this case was to check emails often.

Remember, entering sweepstakes should be a fun and exciting experience because it's easy to get caught up in the chance of entering to win a big prize. After all that is the goal, isn't it? Well, the answer to that can be both Yes and No depending on whom you ask.

For some, winning is everything but for many others the whole process of entering sweepstakes is part of what motivates people and this can be quite addictive. Yet when you dream, you need to remember the old saying that warns you to be careful what you wish for because not all sweepstakes wins are equal nor is it beneficial to win every prize offered. This is extremely easy to say but hard to put into practice.

Top Fifteen
Mail-In Sweepstakes Mistakes

1. Not hand addressing the envelope or postcard.
2. Failing to print information by writing script.
3. Using the wrong size envelope: most sweepstakes specify using a #10 envelope.
4. Using the wrong size card or paper.
5. Photocopying cards, papers or envelopes to enter.
6. Using a printed label on postcards or papers.
7. Not putting the card or paper in an envelope before mailing.
8. Forgetting to seal the envelope.
9. Failing to put postage on the envelope or postcard prior to mailing.
10. Mailing entries either too soon or too late.
11. Using a postcard to enter when a card or paper in an envelope is specified.
12. Mailing all the entries in one envelope versus in separate envelopes.
13. Entering too many times.
14. Entering a sweepstakes targeted toward youth and too old to enter.
15. Not reading the fine print in the rules.

You will note that all these mistakes have in common is a failure to follow the rules.

Social Media and Sweepstakes

One may wonder how sweepstakes existed before the internet. We now have websites, blogs, Facebook™, Twitter™, Instagram™, Pinterest™, YouTube™, Snapchat™, text messaging, and more all offering sweepstakes. Today more than any time in history, people's lives are intertwined with the online world. One point that you might have notice is that many bloggers use the term "giveaway" when in actuality they are in fact running a sweepstakes. Again, they are offering a chance for an individual or individuals to win a prize at random.

As far as social media is concerned, the biggest giant in this arena by far is Facebook™. In February of 2017 Facebook™ reported worldwide monthly activity of 1.86 billion users. Over 66 percent of Facebook™ members use the service daily and over 65 percent use Facebook™ in a mobile fashion. Probably what is most astounding is that there continues to be a double digit increase in use year after year. The implications of this is tremendous and continued growth is huge when it comes to marketing, promotions and of course sweepstakes.

Sponsors have to be very careful on what they require of the entrant. As an example sponsors who use Pinterest™ should not ask contestants to post their contest rules or require individuals to pin the sponsor's product or products, this may be deemed by the Federal Trade Commission an as improper endorsement. Likewise, the requirement of tweeting a specific hashtag may be problematic unless certain disclosures are present.

Note that Facebook™ and Twitter™ forbid individuals from creating multiple accounts for the sole purpose of entering sweepstakes and contests. Your account will be suspended if it is detected. For Facebook™ alone they estimate that 83 million FAKE profiles exist.

Many people might be curious to understand why companies offer sweepstakes and making a point of asking you to click the "Like" or "Share" button? Please note that this cannot be a mandatory requirement to enter for a promotion but companies can still make the request as well as encourage you to opt in and subscribe to allow them to send you further communications.

Well, when you click "Like" you will not see a lot happen on your Facebook™ page, however, this action will be seen listed in your recent activity list and certain web content may also appear in various places such as your friends' and followers' newsfeeds and tickers. Again taking into the fact that so many people are viewing Facebook™ daily makes even a simple "Like" powerful giving the potential eyes that have the opportunity to view this message.

When people choose to "Share" information, the reader decides the message and the social network as well as what picture to use as a thumbnail. This action will place information at the top of your newsfeed and also on all your friends' newsfeeds. From a marketing stand point having someone "Like" your content is good, but having someone "Share" your content is even better because it gives you greater exposure.

Some quick Facebook™ facts that might be of interest are that approximately 30 percent of users are between the ages of 25 to 34 and there are approximately 300 million photo uploads daily and the average time people spend on Facebook™ is twenty minutes.

After reading the above facts, it is easy to understand why marketers want to explore all the options that will enable them to tap in to this huge user base. Sweepstakes and contests have been proven over time to increase interest. Now more than ever you will find companies holding multiple Facebook™ and other social media promotions throughout the year.

Unfortunately, many companies both large and small are still having a difficult time navigating social media platforms and fail to create the exposure or revenue bump they hoped for. There are multiple reasons, but here we would like to expose some of the top deadly mistakes that can turn off consumers which in turn ends promotions before they even get started.

The main reason the promotions fail is companies are requiring a sign-up form that has not been tested and designed properly. In general people don't like filling out forms or disclosing a lot of information about themselves. Another failure in online promotions come from not knowing how to enter. It needs to be simple and straightforward. Many times the barrier to entry is too high. You are asking for too much information when the reward for taking the time and giving that information is perceived to be too low and not worth the effort. Sponsors need to keep in mind that the more difficult it is to enter, the fewer amount of the entries will be received; therefore the prize or prizes offered need to be in line with what is expected. Another reason many company promotions fail is not offering the right prize for the target audience. The prize or prizes need to have a high value proposition. Finally, another mistake is poor marketing which can be both in the initial planning as well as how the promotion was executed. Posting the promotion one time or sending out a few emails is not going to get the results you seek. All these pitfalls and many more are other reasons to hire an agency that has experienced individuals in both marketing and judging sweepstakes and contests.

Code Word Sweepstakes

The world of sweepstakes and promotions are on a continual path of evolution as marketers strive to find new ways to connect with consumers. One way to create excitement and drive traffic is to offer a sweepstakes that requires consumers to find a specific code word that might be displayed during an on-air programming of a television show or located in a print publication, website or even a physical location of the sponsor. Advertisers have found this to be an effective way to create excitement and drive traffic. Some of the most effective code word promotions occur over several weeks and include a daily component offering new prizes but also requiring new codes to keep the consumer engaged. The best code words are those that are short, easy to spell and memorable.

Another use of codes is when an offer is exposed to a limited group, but the media is generalized.

Specifically, HBO™ has a marketing technique of unscrambling the signal for one weekend every year. The idea is that people will see "all they are missing" by not subscribing. To get people to tune in they would send a direct mail offer to many cable subscribers that stated "You may have already won $5,000." Your magic number is 5108. At the conclusion of each movie this weekend you will see a four digit number in red.

"If your number matches, you win!" Only one person got the winning number. The concern was if they called it the winning number all the people that did not get the mailing would call their cable operator and say I want to get number so I can be in the sweepstakes. To circumvent this problem they just ran the number next to the copyright notice with no reference to the offer. Someone that didn't know about the sweepstakes would just assume this number was part of the copyright notice or a movie number.

Second Chance Sweepstakes Drawings

Many times, sweepstakes promotions have game codes that need to be entered in order to win, or they may require consumers to match together game pieces. In these type promotions having a 100 percent redemption rate is difficult, so many times a second chance drawing takes place to award prizes that were not previously redeemed. These second chance drawings are rarely advertised vigorously so this allows those who are watchful a great opportunity to score a win.

Twitter™ Promotions

A few tips about using Twitter™ are to follow the company or person that is holding the contest. Retweet the post that was originally made and make sure it has the hashtag. If there is a Twitter™ Party, join in the fun and participate. Use Twitter™ Search and type in keywords like win prizes, contests or sweepstakes to find promotions you can enter. You might want to consider using TweetDeck™ Twitter™ Client for permanent searches. Think about also looking on your favorite search engines for sites that might list Twitter™ promotions. Again, make sure you are following the brand. It is more difficult for the sponsor to notify you about your winnings if you are not a follower. Finally, make sure to check the rules so you know for certain that retweets are in fact counted as an entry. The following are just a few websites where you can find the latest Twitter™ sweepstakes:

I Love Giveaways: http://www.ilovegiveaways.com/category/twitter

Infinite Sweepstakes: http://www.infinitesweeps.com/sweepstakes/twitter/

Sweepstakes Advantage: https://www.sweepsadvantage.com/twitter-contest.html

Instagram™ Promotions

Instagram™ photo sweepstakes have become popular and the program itself is easy to download and set up. The biggest issue concerning this form of social media is making sure that the photos are original and do not violate any third party rights which include privacy and publicity rights. Likewise, the hashtag itself can be trademarked and the public in some cases have hijacked certain hashtags and take them in a direction that was unintended by the sponsor. To find some of the latest Instagram™ sweepstakes you can visit the following websites:

Infinite Sweepstakes: http://www.infinitesweeps.com/sweepstakes/photo/instagram/

Prize Stakes: http://www.prizestakes.com/sweepstakes/instagram-sweeps/

Texting Promotions

SME which stands for "Short Message Service" or more commonly known as texting is done using a mobile phone. If you enjoy texting, you might want to download a program called Texter™ which helps you create shortcuts to make your texting experience go faster. Before you start texting it is a good idea to check with your cell phone provider and determine, what if any, additional costs are involved.

It is important to note that in 2013 the Telephone Consumer Protection Act was passed which prohibits companies from sending out text messages to your cell phone without first obtaining prior written consent. If a violation occurs and the perpetrator is caught a fine can be levied up to $1,500 per text for violating this statute. This act also applies to calling someone on your cell phone using an auto dialer that tried to leave a pre-record message. There are several exceptions to the law. If a company has a relationship with you, it can send you things like statements or warranty information. Also, non-commercial messages, which includes political surveys or fundraising messages, are also exempt.

Text Message Spam

Text messages often use the promise of free gifts, like computers or gift cards, or product offers, like cheap mortgages, credit cards, or debt relief services to get you to reveal personal information. If you want to claim your gift or pursue an offer, you may need to share personal information, like how much money you make, how much you owe, or your bank account information, credit card number, or Social Security number. Clicking on a link in the message can install malware that collects information from your phone. Once the spammer has your information, it is sold to marketers or, worse, identity thieves.

It can lead to unwanted charges on your cell phone bill. Your wireless carrier may charge you simply for receiving a text message, regardless of whether you requested it.

It can slow cell phone performance by taking up space on your phone's memory.

With all this in mind the following are a few suggestions to help you deal with those unwanted messages you are receiving:

- Delete text messages that ask you to confirm or provide personal information. Legitimate companies don't ask for information like your account numbers or passwords by email or text.
- Don't reply and don't click on links provided in the message. Links can install malware on your computer and take you to spoof sites that look real but whose purpose is to steal your information.
- Treat your personal information like cash. Your Social Security number, credit card numbers, and bank and utility account numbers can be used to steal your money or open new accounts in your name. Don't give them out in response to a text.
- Place your cell phone number on the National Do Not Call Registry.
- If you are an AT&T, T-Mobile, Verizon, Sprint or Bell subscriber, you can report spam texts to your carrier by copying the original message and forwarding it to the number 7726 (SPAM), free of charge.
- Review your cell phone bill for unauthorized charges, and report them to your carrier.

If you receive unwanted commercial text messages, file a complaint with the FTC: https://www.ftccomplaintassistant.gov/Information#crnt&panel1-5

The Federal Communications Commission (FCC) also accepts complaints about unwanted text messages: https://www.fcc.gov/consumers/guides/stop-unwanted-calls-texts-and-faxes

To help you find the latest legitimate text sweepstakes, we suggest you visit the following websites:

Bella's Bog
http://bellasblog.info/text-to-win-games/

Infinite Sweepstakes
http://www.infinitesweeps.com/sweepstakes/text2win/

Instant Win Crazy
http://www.instantwincrazy.com/category/text-to-win/

Sweepstakes Max
http://sweepstakesmax.com/Text_sweeps

Sweeties Sweeps
http://sweetiessweeps.com/category/other-sweeps/text-to-win

Entering Sweepstakes Online

Choosing to enter online is by far the fastest and least expensive way to enter both sweepstakes and contests. However, since it is so easy, there will likely be many more entries. Entering online takes two basic formats. First is the online entry form. With this form you fill out your information and click the respective boxes, many times this will include accepting the official rules and agreeing to abide by them before you are allowed to enter and the form is accepted. The second and extremely popular way to enter is on blogs, websites and social media sites by using applications especially designed for sweepstakes as well as contest giveaways. These applications many times are very inexpensive and easy to use and set up. Now it seems everyone wants to be in the sweepstakes and contest business which can be good for you.

One of the most popular applications you will likely encounter is offered by a company called Woobox™. The company's website touts the application has been used by "over four million brands and collected over one billion entries using Woobox™." Several other application forms are offered by Rafflecopter™ and Viralsweeps™. Again as you enter more and more you will likely see literally hundreds of different applications that all are ready to accept your entry.

There are a few differentiations that need to be pointed out when using applications versus using a standard online website entry form. For some sweepstakes, the number of people who have entered or total number of entrants, may be displayed. While the two might sound the same they are not. With applications there is a long list of actionable steps the sponsor would like you take, such as "Like" their Facebook™ page or "Share" the sweepstakes with your friends. You might also be asked to visit their Pinterest™ page or go to the sponsor's website. All these different individual and independent steps will get you additional entries into the sweepstakes drawing for the prize beyond just clicking to enter. So with this as an example there might only be 100 people who have actually entered the sweepstakes drawing, but in turn each person had the opportunity to have 20 entries if they chose to complete all the steps.

Having this information beforehand is helpful because if you saw that only 50 people entered you might be more apt to enter than if you saw 50,000 people have entered.

Protect Yourself Online

Going online to enter sweepstakes can be fun but not all sweepstakes are legitimate. To protect yourself you need to have multiple antivirus programs on your computer and conduct regular scans frequently to make sure it has not been infected. Several software programs to consider downloading include:

HitmanPro™
https://www.hitmanpro.com/en-us/hmp.aspx

Malwarebytes Anti-Malware™
https://www.malwarebytes.com

Spybot™
https://www.safer-networking.org/

SUPERAntiSpyware™
http://superantispyware.com/index.html

VIPRE™
https://www.vipreantivirus.com/

There are many aspects to consider when entering sweepstakes online. First, you need to recognize that the barrier to entering sweepstakes online is low. Finding sweepstakes to enter is not a problem. In fact there are so many sweepstakes listed that the majority of individuals don't have enough time in their day to enter all the sweepstakes they find. Once you find a sweepstakes you want to enter, the process is easy. Just click the link, read the rules, fill out the online form and submit the link.

Since the amount of time it takes to enter is relatively fast, you can be assured that this process is taking place hundreds, thousands to tens of thousands of times a day depending on the sweepstakes. Just because entering is fast and easy does not mean you should take the time to do it.

Before you enter any sweepstakes there is a series of questions you should ask yourself. Do you really want the prize offered? Can you use the prize? If the prize is valued over $600, which will cause you to receive a 1099-M tax form, are you ready and willing to pay the taxes owed? If you answered yes to all the questions, then click the button to submit your information.

Choosing the amount of time you want to devote to entering sweepstakes online is a personal one. Here are a few tips that will make this task easier and faster.

When many people find a sweepstakes they want to enter more than once, they create a file folder under the tab "Favorites" on the computer. The folder itself might be labeled: My Sweepstakes. Within that folder they then create sub-folders labeled: Daily, Weekly, Monthly, Quarterly, and Unlimited. The sweepstakes link is then saved labeling the link by the end date of the promotion. By setting up this process the individual can create a quicker access to the links. Many people even open up several browser links at one time.

Next, you need to know that there are two software programs that many sweepers use: RoboForm™ https://www.roboform.com/ and Texter™ which can be found by searching online at http://download.cnet.com/windows/. These programs allow you to fill in the online entry blanks faster. Every few minutes you save will help you have more time to enter additional sweepstakes.

So now you have a method in place to load online sweepstakes faster and enter them faster.

Tip: Many people enjoy entering daily sweepstakes online the most because they know that the bulk of the people entering these sweepstakes might only enter one or two times and then stop. However, the avid sweeper who is diligent and has established a system like the one mentioned above will have a greater chance of winning because they will have many more entries.

Sweepstakes Automation

A serious discussion needs to take place when it comes to sweepstakes automation and the official rules. More and more sweepstakes are including in their official rules statements that read:

"Use of any automated system to participate is prohibited and will result in disqualification." Or "The use of automated software or computer programs to register or to enter this Sweepstakes is prohibited and any individual who uses or attempts to use such methods to register or to enter will be disqualified."

So what's this all about anyway? Sponsors running online sweepstakes do so because they are seeking to gain a new or renewed awareness of their products and/or services with the ultimate goal of making more money. Sweepstakes are used as a tool to draw people to their website or Facebook™ page with hopes that the individual will look around and learn more about what the sponsor has to offer.

When you login on your computer and go to a sweepstakes, there is a certain exchange of information that happens automatically. First, the website recognizes how you arrived. Did you get there via an internet search engine or did you type in the URL directly? The website will know the time you logged in as well as what pages you viewed and how long you visited. The server records your IP address which maps out where your computer is located, the type of web browser you are using and your screen resolution.

By using automated software that simply goes to a website to fill out the sweepstakes form and enters it in less than a minute then goes to the next site without human intervention defeats the whole purpose the sponsor had in mind when creating their promotion. So, this is the reason behind placing this statement in the rules notifying users if this type of software or program is used they will be disqualified.

The use of form fillers like RoboForm™ is considered by most to be completely different because using this program still requires human intervention, i.e. a set of eyes looking at the computer screen. However, there is no doubt that most sponsors would prefer individuals spend more time looking at the information they offer versus using anything that speeds up the process.

If the rules specifically say that "manual entry" is required, then you should do so. Manually typing your name and address etc. will take longer than clicking to automatically enter. Remember the website has a time clock so it will know if you took ten seconds or less to enter or several minutes. To defeat the use of an automatic form filling program some sweepstakes are now using a multi-media software platform which requires users to manually keystroke entries.

Sweepstakes Tools for Online Entering

(FREE) "AutoHotkey™ is a free, open-source custom scripting language for Microsoft Windows, initially aimed at providing easy keyboard shortcuts or hotkeys, fast macro-creation and software automation that allows users of most levels of computer skill to automate repetitive tasks in any Windows application" Source: https://www.autohotkey.com/

(FREE) "BUPA™ will allow you to organize, share, display and print UPC codes. This is a very useful program for those who love to enter contests requiring UPC bar codes. If you only have the UPC number, this program will display and print the barcode. Be warned that most contests will not allow a printed barcode for entries. We suggest you print out the barcode and trace it." Source: http://www.emogic.com/store/bupa_free_freeware

(FREE) Fasterfox™ Add-On - For Firefox Browser uses - Saves pages for quick viewing later. Source: https://addons.mozilla.org/en-US/firefox/addon/rsccmanfasterfox/

(FREE) Rewards™ "A simple to use management tool for reward programs, lotteries, contests, etc. List all the Contests, Lotteries and Sites you need to visit regularly. Rewards will notify you when you need to visit the site and it will take you there." Source: http://www.emogic.com/store/rewards_free_freeware

RoboForm™ "Form filling technology allows you to automatically fill in those long, tedious web forms with the simple click of a button. This is ideal for online shopping, entering contests, resume submission and so much more!" Source: http://www.roboform.com/form-filler

(FREE) Sweep™ allows you to track online promotions you enter electronically Sweep Version 1.8 - http://www.wavget.com/download/legacy-downloads/

"Sweepstakes Tracker™ is a total integrated solution for handling all aspects of tracking and entering all types of sweepstakes including online and mail-in. Sweepstakes Tracker's™ advanced features and ease-of-use make it the perfect tool for the casual and serious sweepstaker." Source: http://www.sweepstakestracker.com/

(FREE) Texter™ "Windows only: Text substitution app Texter™ saves you countless keystrokes by replacing abbreviations with commonly used phrases you define. Unlike software-specific text replacement features, Texter™ runs in the Windows™ system tray and works in any application you're typing in. Texter™ can also set return-to markers for your cursor and insert clipboard contents into your replacement text, in addition to more advanced keyboard macros." Source: http://lifehacker.com/238306/lifehacker-code-texter-windows

TweetDeck™ "The most powerful Twitter™ tool for real-time tracking, organizing, and engagement. Reach your audiences and discover the best of Twitter™." Source: https://tweetdeck.twitter.com/

"TypeItIn™ increases your productivity when filling out forms, responding to emails, and many other everyday activities. It also improves your accuracy, greatly reducing rework." Source: http://www.wavget.com/typeitin/

Also, don't forget Google Alerts™ https://www.google.com/alerts. This tool will help notify you when new results from web pages, blogs and more match the search terms you have entered.

Sweepstakes Hobbyist/Professional

No one ever woke up one morning and suddenly became a professional golfer, race car driver or astronaut overnight. Each individual who decided to peruse those avocations knew it was going to take a lot of time, energy and practice in order to be proficient at their respective craft. Secondly, all successful professionals are not only confident in their abilities but pursue their goals with a passion and most importantly keep a positive attitude. People who are negative in life live a self-fulfilling prophecy. If you go around all day telling yourself you will never win, then more than likely this will be the case. However, if you focus on the possible positive outcomes of your efforts, you have a much better chance to succeed. It is important to note that people whom you may identify as professional sweepers only have a winning percentage rate of less than 1 percent of what they enter.

While this might be shocking to some, consider this. Michael Jordan undoubtedly was one of the greatest basketball players of all times. However, during his career he lost 300 games, missed 9,000 shots and missed the game winning shot 26 times. His shooting average was actually below 50 percent. But he is not remembered for this, is he? Another famous person most people recognize is Thomas Edison. In his quest to make the light bulb a success it took him 10,000 attempts. When asked about the other 9,999 times his reply was he had discovered ways that did not work.

Both of these individuals have important qualities that all successful sweepers must possess; accepting failure in a positive light and using that to propel yourself forward versus holding you back. Take everything in stride and realize that entering sweepstakes is a process to be enjoyed versus a job that has to be done. There is a huge lesson to be learned by coming to this realization. Winning is only part of the equation. Professional sweepers don't wait to win; they do all in their power to assure that they will win, but they also realize that winning is just one aspect of this wonderful and exciting hobby.

Sweepstakes Clubs in the US

No matter where you live in the United States, there will likely be a sweepstakes club near you.

It has been estimated that 55 million Americans have entered sweepstakes, many on a regular basis.

Why should you join a club? We all need to be motivated, and while entering sweepstakes can be fun, the fact of the matter is that winning takes time. Joining a club allows you to talk to others and learn about local sweepstakes happening in your area. You will likely pick up a few extra tips to help you win more. Many times clubs will have their own giveaways and set up exchanges for sweepstakes supplies or prizes won that they really don't need or want. Joining a sweepstakes club is a great way to meet a whole new group of friends who share your passion.

To find the most up-to-date information on the club nearest you visit the following websites:

http://www.bestsweepstakes.com/sweepstakesclubs.html

http://contestqueen.com/us-resources/meet-fellow-sweepers/sweepstakes-clubs/

http://www.sweepsadvantage.com/forum/sweepstakes-clubs/index6.html

http://www.sweepsheet.com/clubs.ashx

Online Sweepstakes Social Clubs

This N' That Sweepstakes Club is a monthly newsletter published and edited by Carol McLaughlin and you can email her at: tnte-mail@comcast.net

What makes this publication different is that it does not provide specific information on any sweepstakes but rather serves as a valuable means of socializing with others in the hobby.

SWAP Newsletter - SWAP is all about "Sharing With A Pal" edited by Linda Clineman and you can email her at: SWAP4FunNL@gmail.com

SWAP is a monthly publication for friendly Member 2 Member drawings & giveaways.

Sweepstakes Newsletters

Sweepstakes newsletters are a great source to find new sweepstakes that are being offered to consumers. However, simply subscribing to these newsletters doesn't guarantee you to be a winner. Regardless, most people who are serious about winning subscribe to one or more newsletters to supplement what they find to enter online.

Another benefit to subscribing is reading additional tips about entering and stories from others who have won. Reading these success stories is helpful because it gives sweepers a boost during those dry spells everyone experiences when winning something seems to be almost impossible.

Best Sweepstakes Newsletter
PO Box 1882
Venice, FL 34284
Website: http://www.bestsweepstakes.com/

For over 20 years Best Publications™ has been supplying valuable information to those interested in entering mail-in sweepstakes. There are multiple newsletter subscription options available to fit any budget. Members receive information either by email or postal mail as often as weekly or monthly if they prefer.

Best Publications™ also offer a free online sweepstakes section which lists single entry sweepstakes and sweepstakes that offer trips, cash, autos, electronics and more. This list can be found online at: http://www.bestsweepstakes.com/onlinesweeps.html

iWinContests
PO Box 1963
Minneola, FL 34755
Website: http://iwincontests.com/

Tom Cavalli is the driving force behind iWinContests.com an online sweepstakes newsletter. You will find Tom at most regional and national sweepstakes conventions. For him finding and entering sweepstakes has turned into a lifelong passion. His first big win was at age five winning an Atari at Burger King. Since then his devotion to the hobby has paid off big time earning him over 40 trips including one prize package worth over $150,000 that sent him to Brazil for the World Cup™ with the USA Men's National Soccer Team!

The email newsletter is delivered every Thursday evening, contains lots of clickable links to many of the lesser known sweepstakes most with short entry windows that are not mentioned in other newsletters. His newsletter has an "Act Now" section as well as a section devoted to text sweepstakes. He also offers a 30-day money back guarantee: "If for any reason you don't see value in our product, simply email us and request a refund. No questions asked." This is one publication you don't want to pass up!

Online-Sweepstakes.com (OLS)
P.O. Box 157
Springfield, OH 45501-0157
Website: http://www.online-sweepstakes.com

This website is free to register and offers individuals the opportunity to click and enter several thousand sweepstakes. You also can also subscribe to the OLS Premium Membership. The premium membership gives members another thousand sweepstakes to enter, many offering better prizes.

Sweeping America
P.O. Box 211
Broken Arrow, OK 74013-0211
Website: http://sweepingamerica.com/

Sweeping America is a newsletter that is delivered weekly by email or online at least thirty new snail mail sweepstakes.

Sweep-Easy http://www.sweep-easy.com/

Sweep-Easy subscriptions receive a weekly email that contains a list of approximately 350 daily sweepstakes. Also included will be the sweepstakes rules and the end date for the sweepstakes.

SweepSheet http://www.sweepsheet.com/

SweepSheet is a sweepstakes publication edited by Patti Osterheld. Each new issue is placed online or sent my mail every two weeks and contains on average 37 new sweepstakes.

Sweepstakes Master File Listing

The internet is constantly changing and sometimes websites become abandoned and are no longer updated. To find the latest information on the Sweepstakes List - Master File visit: www. SweepstakesExpert.com. Below is a list of over 120 sweepstakes and contests websites. These links will give you access to a multitude of different sweepstakes and contests you can enter to win hundreds of thousands of dollars in cash and prizes.

1sweepstakes.com: http://1sweepstakes.com/

Ace Contests: http://www.acecontests.com/

All American Sweepstakes: http://www.allamericansweepstakes.com/

Lucky Day: http://anyluckyday.com/

Bellas Blog: http://bellasblog.info/

Bella Online(sm): http://www.bellaonline.com/misc/sweeps/

Best Sweepstakes: http://www.bestsweepstakes.com/

BigSweeps Sweepstakes: http://www.bigsweeps.com/welcome.cfm

Classic Heartland: http:/www.classicheartland.com/

Contests.about: http://contests.about.com/

Contests and Giveaways: http://contestsgiveaways.com/

Contest Bank: http://www.contestbank.com/

Contest Bee: http://www.contestbee.com/

Contest Chest: http://contestchest.com/

Contest Cook: http://www.contestcook.com/index.html

Contest Girl: http://www.contestgirl.com/

Contest Listing: http://www.contestlisting.com/

Contest Mob Blog: http://www.contestmob.com/blog/

Contest Queen: http://contestqueen.com/fromthe/

Contest Scoop: https://contestscoop.com/win-cash/

Contest Share: http://contestshare.com/

ContestforMoms.com: http://www.contestformoms.com/

Cooking Contest Central: https://cookingcontestcentral.com/

Coupon Clipinista: https://www.facebook.com/CouponClipinista/

Coupon Pro: http://www.couponproblog.com/sweepstakes/

Eighty MPH Mom: http://eightymphmom.com/category/reviews-giveaways

Enter Online Sweepstakes: http://enteronlinesweeps.com/

Enter To Win Contests: http://www.entertowincontests.com/

Everyday Family: http://www.everydayfamily.com/sweepstakes/

EnterToWin: https://myentertowin.com/car-sweepstakes-giveaways

Fatwallet.com: https://www.fatwallet.com/forums/contests-and-sweepstakes/

Fishbowl Prizes: http://www.fishbowlprizes.com/

Free 4 Him: http://free4him.com/

Free Booksy: https://www.freebooksy.com/

Freebie Mom: https://freebiemom.com/sweepstakes/

FreebieShark.com: http://www.freebieshark.com/sweepstakes

Free Prize Giveaways: http://www.freeprizegiveaways.com/

Free Stuff Times: http://www.freestufftimes.com/contests/

Giveaway Frenzy: http://giveawayfrenzy.com/

GiveawayJunkie.com: http://giveawayjunkie.com/

GiveawayMonkey: http://www.giveawaymonkey.com/

Giveaway Promote: http://www.giveawaypromote.com/

Giveawaytoday.net: https://giveawaytoday.net/

GiveawayUS.com: http://giveawayus.com/

Good Reads: http://www.goodreads.com/giveaway

Hip2Save: http://hip2save.com/category/get-rewarded/sweepstakes/

Hunt4Freebies: http://hunt4freebies.com/

Hypersweep: http://www.hypersweep.com/

I Love Giveaways: http://www.ilovegiveaways.com/

Infinite Sweepstakes: http://www.infinitesweeps.com/

Instant Win Crazy: http://www.instantwincrazy.com/

iNeverWinAnything: http://www.ineverwinanything.com/

Julie's Freebies http://juliesfreebies.com/

Just Sweep: http://justsweep.com/

KW: http://www.kidzworld.com/contests

LaPrima Royale: http://laprimaroyale.com/

Last Chance Sweepstakes: http://www.lastchancesweepstakes.com/

Lucky Contests - Sweepstakes: http://www.luckycontests.com/

Mr. Free Stuff: http://www.mrfreestuff.com/

Mrs. Sweepstakes: http://www.mrssweepstakes.com/

MySaving.com: https://www.mysavings.com/free-sweepstakes-contests-giveaways/

Offers Contest: http://www.offerscontest.com/

Online-Sweepstakes.com: http://www.online-sweepstakes.com/

Our Instant Win: http://www.ourinstantwin.com/

Online sweepstakes: https://www.pinterest.com/explore/online-sweepstakes/

Penniless Teacher: http://pennilessteacher.com/

PrizeGrab.com: http://prizegrab.com/sweepstakes/free/

Prizestakes: http://www.prizestakes.com/

Reddit Sweepstakes: https://www.reddit.com/r/sweepstakes/

RewardIt: http://sweepstakes.rewardit.com/

SandysRealm.com Sweepstakes: http://www.sandysrealm.com/

Savings Secrets: http://www.savingsecrets.com/sweepstakes

Share Your Freebies: http://shareyourfreebies.com/category/sweepstakes/

Slickdeals.net: http://slickdeals.net/forums/forumdisplay.php?f=25

Snazzywin.com: http://snazzywin.com/

SWAGHUB: http://sweepstakesandgiveawayshub.com/

Sweepon: http://www.sweepon.com/

Sweeping To Win: https://www.sweepingtowin.com/

Sweeps Maniac: http://www.sweepsmaniac.com/

Sweepstakes: http://mysweepstakescontests.com/

Sweepstake.com: http://www.sweepstake.com/

Sweepstakes Alerts: http://sweepstakesalerts.com/

Sweepstakes Advantage: http://www.sweepsadvantage.com/

SweepstakesBible: http://www.sweepstakesbible.com/

Sweepstakes Bug: http://www.sweepstakesbug.com/

Sweepstakes Crazy: http://www.sweepstakescrazy.com/

SweepstakesDaily.com: http://www.sweepstakesdaily.com/

Sweepstakes Fanatics: http://www.sweepstakesfanatics.com/

SweepstakesGuide.com: http://www.sweepstakesguide.com/

Sweepstakes in Seattle: https://sweepstakesinseattle.com/

Sweepstakes Lovers: http://www.sweepstakeslovers.com/

SweepstakesMag: http://www.sweepstakesmag.com/

SweepStakesMania.com: http://www.sweepstakesmania.com/

Sweepstakes Max: http://sweepstakesmax.com/

Sweepstaking.net: http://www.sweepstaking.net/

Sweepstakes Plus: https://www.sweepstakesplus.com/

Sweepstakes-Search.com: http://www.sweepstakes-search.com/

SweepstakesToday.com: http://www.sweepstakestoday.com/

Sweepstown: http://www.sweeptown.com/-sweepstakes/

Sweeties Sweeps: http://sweetiessweeps.com/

Teen.com: http://www.teen.com/category/freebies-and-sweepstakes/

The Balance: https://www.thebalance.com/complete-contests-and-sweepstakes-list-887113

The Contests Center: http://www.contestcen.com/

TheFreeSite.com: http://www.thefreesite.com/Prizes_and_Contests/

UltraContest.com: http://www.ultracontest.com/

USA Contests Online: http://www.usacontestsonline.com/

USA Freebies Daily: http://usafreebiesdaily.com/

Win A Sweepstakes: http://winasweepstakes.com/

Win A Sweepstakes – Pinterest: https://www.pinterest.com/winasweepstakes/

Win A Sweepstakes – Twitter: https://twitter.com/WinASweepstakes

Win Prizes Online: http://www.winprizesonline.com/

Win Prizes Online – Facebook: https://www.facebook.com/WinPrizesOnline

Winzilly: https://www.winzily.com/topics/sweepstakes/

WomenFreebies.com: https://womanfreebies.com/

Whole Mom: http://www.wholemom.com/

Your Contests USA: http://www.yourcontests.us/

Yes U Won Sweepstakes and Contests: http://www.yesuwon.com/

International Competitions

Giveaway & Contests: http://www.internationalgiveaway.com/

Canada

Ace Contests: http://www.acecontests.com/

Canadian Contests Online:
http://www.canadacontestsonline.com/

Canadian Free Stuff:
http://www.canadianfreestuff.com/canadian-contests/

Contest Canada.net: http://www.contestcanada.net/

Contest Girl: http://www.contestgirl.com/

LookContests.com: http://lookcontests.com/

Free.ca: http://free.ca/contests/

Sweepstakes.ca: http://www.sweepstakes.ca/

Win a Contest: http://www.winacontest.com/

South Africa

Just Play: http://www.justplay.co.za/

Win Prizes: https://www.win-prizes.co.za/

United Kingdom

Ace Contests: http://www.acecontests.com/

The Prize Finder: https://www.theprizefinder.com/

Magazine and Other Online Sweepstakes

Below you will find over 130 magazines and other online sites that offer sweepstakes and/or contests you can enter.

It should be noted that not all magazine sweepstakes offerings are exactly as they might appear. An example would be a sweepstakes listing a cash prize of $100,000. In most cases these larger dollar prizes are actually being advertised on the multiple magazine websites owned by the same parent company. So only one prize is given away not 10 or 20 as it might appear.

It is important to make sure when entering magazine sweepstakes you look closely before clicking the submit button. Many magazines list sweepstakes on a separate promotional page in an effort to generate new magazine subscriptions. However, note there should always be an option to enter any sweepstakes without having to subscribe. Again, as with all sweepstakes, make sure you read the official rules and look carefully over the information before you enter.

American Media Inc.

Star Magazine: http://starmagazine.com/category/sweepstakes/

OK Magazine: http://okmagazine.com/sweepstakes/

Bauer Magazine L.P. Sweepstakes

ABC Soaps In Depth: http://winit.abc.soapsindepth.com/sweepstakes/

Animal Tales: http://winit.animaltalesmag.com/sweepstakes/

Astro Girl Freebies: http://winit.astrogirlfreebies.com/sweepstakes/

CBS Soaps In Depth: http://winit.cbs.soapsindepth.com/sweepstakes/

Closer Weekly: http://winit.closerweekly.com/sweepstakes/

FHM: http://winit.fhm.com/sweepstakes/

First For Woman: http://winit.firstforwomen.com/sweepstakes/

Girls' World: http://winit.girlsworldmag.com/

Ideas and Discoveries: http://winit.ideasanddiscoveries.com/sweepstakes/

In Touch Weekly: http://winit.intouchweekly.com/sweepstakes/

J-14: http://winit.j-14.com/sweepstakes/

Life and Styles Weekly: http://winit.lifeandstylemag.com/sweepstakes/

M Magazine: http://winit.m-magazine.com/sweepstakes/

More: http://win.more.com/

Now To Love: http://winit.nowtolove.com.au/

Quiz Fest: http://winit.quizfest.com/sweepstakes/

Sweepon: http://www.sweepon.com/sweepstakes/

Twist Magazine: http://winit.twistmagazine.com/sweepstakes/

Woman's World: http://winit.womansworld.com/sweepstakes/

Boy Scouts of America

Boy's Life: http://boyslife.org/giveaways/

CBS Studios Inc.

Entertainment Tonight: http://www.etonline.com/giveaways/

The Talk: http://www.cbs.com/shows/the_talk/giveaways/

CityScene Media Group

CityScene: http://www.citomycenecolumbus.com/giveaways/contests

Clevver Network

Teen.com: http://www.teen.com/category/freebies-and-sweepstakes/

Condé Nast

Allure: http://www.allure.com/topic/sweepstakes

Architectural Digest: http://www.architecturaldigest.com/

Bon Appetit: http://www.bonappetit.com/collection/promotions

Brides: http://bridesallaccess.com/sweepstakes.asp

Condé Nast Traveler: http://www.cntraveller.com/news/competitions

Glamour: http://www.glamour.com/about/sweepstakes

GQ: http://www.gq.com/about/giveaway

Self: http://promotions.self.com

Teen Vogue: http://www.teenvogue.com/search?q=sweepstakes

The New Yorker: http://contest.newyorker.com

The Enthusiast Network

AnalogPlanet: http://www.analogplanet.com/category/sweepstakes

AudioStream: http://www.audiostream.com/category/sweepstakes

InnerFidelity: http://www.innerfidelity.com/category/sweepstakes

Shutter Bug: http://www.shutterbug.com/category/sweepstakes

Sound & Vision: http://www.soundandvision.com/category/sweepstakes

Sterophile: http://www.stereophile.com/category/sweepstakes

F+W Media

How: http://www.howdesign.com/design-competitions/

Popular Woodwork Magazine:
http://www.popularwoodworking.com/popular-woodworking-sweepstakes

The Artists Magazine: http://www.artistsnetwork.com/category/competitions

Girls' Life Acquisition Co

Girls' Life: http://www.girlslife.com/free-stuff

Grand View Media

Grand View Outdoors: http://www.grandviewoutdoors.com/sweepstakes/

HarperCollins Publishers

Epic Reads: http://www.epicreads.com/contest/

Harpo, Inc.

Omag Online: http://omagonline.com/win-it.php

The Doctor Oz Show: http://www.doctoroz.com/giveaways

Heartlight Girls Publications, LLC

BYOU "Be Your Own You" Magazine: https://www.byoumagazine.com/prizes

Hearst Online Magazine Sweepstakes

Best Products: http://www.bestproducts.com/sweepstakes-giveaways/

Cosmopolitan: http://cosmopolitan.hearstmobile.com/sweeps_and_contests/

Country Living: http://countryliving.hearstmobile.com/sweeps/

Dr. Oz The Good Life: http://doctorozmag.hearstmobile.com/sweeps/

ELLE: http://elle.hearstmobile.com/Sweepstakes/

ELLE DÉCOR: http://elledecor.hearstmobile.com/giveaways/

Esquire: http://esquire.hearstmobile.com/sweeps/

Food Network Magazine: http://www.foodnetwork.com/features/articles/sweepstakes-and-contests.html

Good Housekeeping: http://goodhousekeeping.hearstmobile.com/sweeps/

Harper's BAZAAR: http://harpersbazaar.hearstmobile.com/giveaways/

HGTV Magazine: http://www.hgtvmagonline.com/sweepstakes

House Beautiful: http://housebeautiful.hearstmobile.com/giveaways/

Marie Claire: http://www.marieclaire.com/sweepstakes/

O, The Oprah Magazine: http://www.oprah.com/app/sweepstakes.html

Popular Mechanics: http://popularmechanics.hearstmobile.com/sweeps/

Redbook: http://redbook.hearstmobile.com/online-sweepstakes/

Road & Track: http://roadandtrack.hearstmobile.com/sweeps/

Seventeen: http://seventeen.hearstmobile.com/fun/freebies/

Town & Country: http://townandcountry.hearstmobile.com/giveaways/

Veranda: http://www.veranda.com/sweepstakes/

Woman's Day: http://womansday.hearstmobile.com/giveaways/

Latina Media Ventures LLC

Latina: http://www.latina.com/freebies-sweepstakes-giveaways-deals

Leite's Culinaria, Inc.

http://leitesculinaria.com/category/giveaways

May Media Group, LLC.

KIWI Magazine: http://www.kiwimagonline.com/category/goodies/contests-sweepstakes-and-giveaways/

Meredith Corporation

Better Homes and Gardens: http://www.bhg.com/sweepstakes/

Eating Well: http://promo.eatingwell.com/category/sweeps-offers/

Family Circle: http://my.familycircle.com/sweepstakes/

Family Fun: http://www.parents.com/familyfunpromo/funfinder/

Fit Pregnancy and Baby: http://www.fitpregnancy.com/sweepstakes/

Fitness: http://my.fitnessmagazine.com/sweepstakes/

Martha Stewart: http://www.marthastewart.com/sweepstakes/

Midwest Living: http://my.midwestliving.com/sweepstakes/

More: https://win.more.com/

Parents: http://www.parents.com/sweepstakes/

Rachael Ray Everyday: http://my.rachaelraymag.com/sweepstakes/

Recipe: http://www.recipe.com/sweepstakes/

Shape: https://win.shape.com/

Modern Cat, Inc.

Modern Cat: http://moderncat.com/giveaways

Modern Dog, Inc.

Modern Dog: http://moderndogmagazine.com/giveaways

Ogden Publications, Inc.

Mother Earth News: http://www.motherearthnews.com/ogden_contests

Mother Earth Living: http://www.motherearthliving.com/ogden_contests

Utne Reader: http://www.utne.com/ogden_contests

Grit: http://www.grit.com/ogden_contests

Capper's Farmer: http://www.cappersfarmer.com/ogden_contests

Farm Collector: http://www.farmcollector.com/ogden_contests

Motorcycle Classics: http://www.motorcycleclassics.com/ogden_contests

Group One Enterprises

SWAT Magazine: http://www.swatmagazinegiveaways.com/

June Media, Inc.

BetterRecipes: http://win.betterrecipes.com/

Reunions Magazine Inc.

Reunions Magazine: http://www.reunionsmag.com/resources/resources_contests.html

RFP Corp

Bridal Guide: http://www.bridalguide.com/sweepstakes

Refinery29

Refinery29: http://www.refinery29.com/contests

Rodale, Inc.

Men's Health: http://www.menshealth.com/tags/sweepstakes

Scripps Networks Interactive, Inc.

Asian Food Channel
http://www.asianfoodchannel.com/search?q=contests&t=&p=

DIY Network
http://www.diynetwork.com/about-us/diy-sweepstakes

Food Network
http://www.foodnetwork.com/features/articles/sweepstakes-and-contests.html

Great America Country http://www.greatamericancountry.com/about-us/sweepstakes

HGTV: http://www.hgtv.com/about-us/hgtv-sweepstakes?ic1=utilitysweeps

Travel Channel: http://www.travelchannel.com/sweepstakes

Scrubs, Inc.

Scrubs Magazine: http://scrubsmag.com/giveaways/

Stovall Media, Inc.

Sportsman's Gear Magazine: http://www.sportsmansgearmag.com/sweepstakes

Time Inc.

All You: http://www.allyou.com/sweepstakes/sweepstakes-giveaways

Coastal Living: http://www.coastalliving.com/general/sweepstakes

Cooking Light: http://www.cookinglight.com/marketplace/sweepstakes

Cozi: http://www.cozi.com/freebies-downloads/

Food & Wine: http://www.foodandwine.com/promo

Health: http://www.health.com/health/wp/0%2C%2C20483796%2C00.html

My Home Ideas: http://www.myhomeideas.com/sweepstakes

Real Simple: https://www.realsimple.com/magazine-and-more/inside-website/contests-sweepstakes

Southern Living: http://www.southernliving.com/marketplace/sweepstakes

Sunset: http://www.sunset.com/marketplace/sweepstakes

Trusted Media Brands, Inc.

Birds & Bloom: http://www.birdsandblooms.com/contest-promotions/

Country: http://www.country-magazine.com/contests/

Country Woman: http://www.countrywomanmagazine.com/contests-giveaways/

Farm & Ranch Living: http://www.farmandranchliving.com/contests/

Reader's Digest: http://www.rd.com/sweepstakes-prizes/

Remnisce: http://www.reminisce.com/contests/

Taste Of Home: http://www.tasteofhome.com/

The Family Handyman: https://www.familyhandyman.com/contests-promotions

Warner Bros. Entertainment

Extra TV: http://extratv.com/giveaways/

Weider Publications, LLC

Muscle & Fitness: http://www.muscleandfitness.com/features/sweeps-giveaways

Prizes

Do you REALLY want to win all the prizes offered or at the very least have someone you might want to give them to as a gift? Another way to ask this question is how desirable is this prize? It is understandable that most people enjoy the thrill of "winning something" versus just winning a bigger prize on rare occasions, but it makes no sense to waste your time or money to enter for prizes you don't really want or need - even if they are free. Remember, everyone's resources, be it both time and money, are limited so what you might think is free may actually be costing you in the long run. This brings you to the next important question that you need to consider. Can you afford to win the prize and pay the required taxes? If not, then how easy will it be for you to sell the prize? Finally, you need to take into consideration the probability of you actually winning. Many people in this hobby never really seriously consider the odds of winning. This is a critical mistake. In order to win more you need to focus your energy on sweepstakes where you have a greater chance to win than entering those one in a million shots in the dark.

Tee-shirts, water bottles, coupons for free chocolate bars are all fun prizes to win, but are these prizes worth the postage or even the time you might be spending on the internet trying to win them? Time is a valuable commodity that cannot be replaced so you need to make sure all the effort you make is achieving what you ultimately wish to accomplish.

Entering sweepstakes should be a fun hobby versus something that brings on stress. Filling out forms or mailing in entries and dreaming about winning should be part of your fun that helps create the motivation and excitement to want to continue. Most people enjoy the rush of adrenaline when they find out they have won. But like any hobby, you can't expect to achieve success unless you work at it. Many people get excited when they first start entering sweepstakes which is normal.

What separates the novice from the more serious individual is understanding that winning takes time and perseverance. Your first big win might be weeks, months or even years away. Oftentimes you will hear folks who are avid sweepers talk about the three "P's", i.e. patience, perseverance and positive attitude. Previously the last "P" was for postage but now many people have switched to entering online for free to save money. All these are attributes you must possess in order to be successful in this hobby.

Why are Certain Prizes Offered?

Most people these days have a driver's license and know the basics of how to drive a vehicle. However, few people know the actual mechanics in detail of how the vehicle they drive actually works. The same can be said with sweepstakes. You might understand the process of how to enter, but it is also important that you know much more than just how to click a mouse, affix a stamp, text, tweet or pin.

When you think of the word "promotion," you need to understand in simple terms this is just one type of business strategy used in marketing a company's product or service. The overall goal of running promotions is basically twofold. First, to create a consumer awareness and second and most important, to bring about a reaction in the consumer that triggers an interest and demand for the product or service being advertised. It should then be easy to see that companies have expectations when implementing promotional activity that this will indeed help drive sales of a company's goods and/or services. In addition, there are many other reasons companies run sweepstakes. They want to make an offer that will get stores to build a display around their product. They may want to create a PR event or possibly to draw attention to an anniversary. Of course, in the final analysis it comes down to selling more product. It's been said a sweepstakes is like a brass band at a parade; simply a way to draw attention to an advertisement and or a product.

When you enter sweepstakes you will no doubt notice that many times the prizes offered will often be branded with the corporate logo or possibly the mascot of the product, if there is one. Maybe you have wondered, "Why?" So here is the answer.

The promotional product industry is huge totaling more than $17 billion. When you think of items that are used in promoting a product or service it can be almost anything from a simple ballpoint pen to a baseball cap, tee shirt or much, much more. These advertising premiums or incentives are part of an overall marketing strategy to increase brand awareness and promote a positive impression of the brand. You might be wondering how prevalent promotional products are in our daily lives. Well, looking at industry reports you will find that within the last 12 months approximately 88 percent of the average American consumer will acknowledge having received some type of promotional product. Likewise, over half of these consumers will give a favorable impression of the advertiser after they receive this product. Around 47 percent of the people keep the product they received for more than a year. Also, it is worth mentioning that more than half of the people will use the promotional product they have received once a week or more and surprisingly one in four people will actually carry the promotional item on their person. With the above facts, it is easy to understand why companies seem eager to offer these types of generally low cost items in a promotion. They want their brand to be not only seen but remembered by the consumer.

What Happens to Unclaimed Prizes?

It is not unusual for some sweepstakes prizes to go unclaimed. You might think that the judges keep these prizes, give them away to friends, or return them to the original company. Not so. Usually the judging firm will hold another drawing and distribute unclaimed prizes to other people who have mailed in their entry forms. This is done for the safety of the judging company as well as for you. It means that no prizes will go unclaimed. It eliminates the frequent worry on the part of consumers that prizes in sweepstakes are not actually given away.

Some companies take extra precautions to make sure that no mistakes are made. One company sends out a congratulation letter to the grand-prize winner, and then spends months double-checking all other winning entries. Then they send out the other prizes including everything from lowly free product coupons to $5,000-cash prizes, automobiles, television sets, and cameras. If you are a winner, you will be notified by mail. If you don't receive a letter, and you want to find out who the big winners were in the sweepstakes, you can get a list from the company about five months after the winners have been announced. This way they double-check and you double-check. It would be a real pity to miss out just from carelessness.

How are Winners Selected?

Everybody is eligible to win, and everybody has the same chance. You might still be asking, "How is this possible?" How are mail in entries and electronic entries treated the same?

Recently, an article ("How Does HGTV™ Choose Its Dream Home Winners?") answering this exact question:

This was a great question considering that there were over 94 million entries! How this agency handled this massive amount of entries was not necessarily unique but does give individuals a glimpse into how the process can work. In short, all the entries were divided into bins - be it actual for mail-in entries or virtual bins for electronic entries. Each bin held 50,000 entries. Next, this company used ping pong balls and a hopper. They wrote all the bin numbers both real and virtual on individual ping pong balls and mixed them up in the hopper and drew out the winning bin number. The next step involved choosing the potential qualifying winner from the bin. In the case of a virtual bin number being selected, a computer program would be used to cycle through all the entries that qualified so quickly they could not be read and then a button would be pressed to stop the cycle to choose a winner. In the case of an actual bin number being selected, the bin would be pulled and entries dumped on the floor. An individual would be blindfolded and then sent into the pile of entries to select the potential winner, if they qualified, meaning that they filled out all the necessary information on their entry.

It should be worth noting that the above example was how that particular agency handled that specific drawing so other agencies may use a different method. Generally, however, with the smaller sweepstakes, mail arrives from the post office in mail bags and depending on the size of the agency is sorted and stacked in the mail room. Sometimes the bags are numbered and sometimes they are not. A random bag is selected and someone reaches in and pulls out an envelope or postcard. If the entry has followed the rules and all the information appears on the entry it is declared the winner. Often additional entries are pulled in case the first entry cannot be contacted, or they do not fill out and turn back in the paperwork needed in time or if they decline the prize offered.

In other sweepstakes entries are assigned a number in the order they are received and a random number generator is used to pick the winning numbers.

Still in other sweepstakes that may occur online winning times are chosen in advance and the entry that comes closest to matching the winning time wins.

Since winners are chosen at random there is no real strategy you can use to improve your odds with one exception. If the sweepstakes allows you to enter more than one time, then the more entries you enter the better your odds.

Why Am I Not Winning?

Sometimes people entering sweepstakes have a misconception that once they start entering sweepstakes they will automatically start winning big. Sweepers all wish it was that simple, but unfortunately it isn't. This hobby requires individuals to not only be patient but have perseverance and know that your time will come if you remain steady. Unfortunately, many people give up quickly before they really get started. Regardless, it is helpful to at least understand some of the common reasons why people don't win.

The biggest factor in people not winning is due to the fact that their entries are disqualified. People fail to read the rules, and they ignore the beginning and end dates of the promotion and much more. It is important to follow all rules so your entry is not eliminated on a technicality. If the rules ask for the entry to be on a postcard and you mail in a 3"x 5" card you will be disqualified.

There are always folks that say "How come I never win?" Usually when asked "Do you enter?" they sheepishly say "Well, no."

Mr. Feinman recently spoke at a hobbyist convention. An elderly gentleman came up and said "I can't believe I never win." When asked if he entered he said "Yes, all the time." At which time he produced a box of 500 envelopes. He said I have entered over 5,000 times. In fact here's five hundred entries I am about to mail today. He started to take out the envelopes. Each was neatly computer printed with the address of a major mail in sweepstakes. Each had a forever stamp. When asked had he read the rules He said "of course."

Next I said, "I know this particular sweepstakes the rules say 'Handprint the entry envelope.'" He replied, "Well, my son is in the computer business so to save time I have him computer print envelopes and print my name an address inside." Sadly this person had spent thousands on postage and had no chance of winning. *When I explained he would never win if he didn't f*ollow the rules, He said, "that's silly." I said he may be silly but you have no chance of winning as long as you insist on entering the way you do.

Simple mistakes with your street address including not providing your zip code as well as failing to provide your email address happens frequently. If the judging agency is distributing hundreds or even thousands of prizes to winners, they are not going to take the time to look up your zip code. It is easier to disqualify your entry for not providing all the information required. Also, it is not uncommon for a winning notification email to get blocked and end up in a spam email folder that is rarely checked.

Another common mistake happens when a winning notification email is sent to the individual and they fail to check their email often and another winner is chosen because the time to respond has expired. Lastly, a big reason for people not winning is because they are not entering enough. Occasionally, a winner might just send in one or two entries into sweepstakes that allow multiple entries but more consistent winners are known to send in a hundred to three hundred entries per day. Yes, you read that correctly. Even with this huge number of entries these individuals are reporting that they on average win between five to fifteen prizes per month or less than 1 percent of what they entered.

How to Avoid Sweepstakes Burnout

It is extremely easy to get caught up in the moment and excitement of entering sweepstakes. However, as weeks become months and no winning letter or emails show up you can't help but begin to wonder and a little doubt starts creeping in. At first you try to ignore it then your mind starts to tell you that you have probably been wasting your time and money. This is all common and happens to nearly every person who has entered sweepstakes at one time or another. So how do you break out of this funk? Well, first you need to remind yourself of the old adage that "Rome was not build in a day," and winning a sweepstakes will not happen overnight. This is why it is extremely important that you keep what you are doing in perspective and enjoy the process as much as you enjoy the positive results.

EVERY person who is serious about sweeping needs to create a scrapbook or at the very least have a box with papers that can serve as a reminder of their prior wins.

When you find yourself feeling down about not having much success lately, stop and get up and grab a cold beverage and look through your scrapbook or box and relive those moments from past wins. I realize when you are starting out you might not have anything to show for your effort right now, but you will soon. Just keep going and don't give up. Another thing you might want to do is text, email or call another fellow sweeper and whine a little and get it off your chest. It is ok to be frustrated but the key is not to let it consume you but make you try just a little bit harder.

What Makes a Winner Win?

If you ever get the opportunity then you need to attend at least one national or regional sweepstakes conventions that is held each year. Events have been on the west coast, east coast, and even on the high seas. At these conventions you will get to see and hear from some of the actual winners themselves. There is something that is magical and energizing when you get in a room with several hundred people who all have a passion for winning. People of all ages and walks of life are in attendance. The vast majority of sweepers tend to be women and older versus younger. People are friendly and most are willing to tell you a few stories of what they have won. Eventually, you will hear mentioned the terminology concerning winning the 4 C's. "What's that," you might ask? Well, if you are a diehard sweeper one of the many goals you hope one day to achieve is to win a car, computer, cruise and of course the prize people like the most, cash.

At some point during the national sweepstakes convention there is always a call for the audience to participate by standing, letting everyone see who has won one of the 4 C's namely a car or some other vehicle. People are generally shocked to see all the folks standing. Next they will ask the people to remain standing if you have won two, three and so on. It is amazing as well as inspiring to see how many people are still standing when the numbers keep climbing. At one convention one person remained standing that won a total of 14 vehicles! Another C that gains a lot of attention is cash. At that same convention another individual had won a million dollar prize! As far as trips go, you can just ask anyone sitting at your table, and you will likely hear people talking about dozens of trips to many locations all over the world.

By attending one of these conventions you will literally feel the energy. Beyond these fascinating stories you will meet many friendly people from all over the country. You will learn what motivates them and hear so many wonderful stories.

A sweepstakes convention would not be a convention if they did not give away prizes as well. Another one of the C's (computers) are often on the list as one of the many prizes given away during these multi-day conferences. You can expect to hear people winning hundreds of dollars in postage, gift cards as well as cash and yes, even the potential for a car.

You will find a common thread among most successful sweepers. The first that stands out above the rest is their attitude. Sweepers for the most part are optimistic people who see challenges as potential opportunities versus unmovable obstacles. In short, what sets winners apart from losers is their attitude. An important rule most avid sweepstakes winners follow is to be happy for the winner even if it is not you.

In order to attain the 4 C's of sweepstakes, you have to be a master of the three "P's." This begins with having the positive outlook, closely followed by being patient and finally by being persistent. Winners are realistic individuals who accept the fact that while they might not win every time, they know that they will win soon.

Many years ago in the 1980s then D.L. Blair president, Tom Conlon, was once recorded as saying, there is a "monomaniacal" contingent of about fifteen thousand professional entrants whose names appear over and over in judging records who seem to enter everything.

Without a doubt many of the people attending these sweepstakes conventions are very successful at winning; however, realize that most people entering sweepstakes do so as a hobby versus a profession. Regardless, sweepstakes winners are people who work hard at what they do. Just because entering sweepstakes is considered a hobby does not in any way mean people are not serious about what they are doing.

You will find many people who win a lot of prizes end up being very generous with their winnings and commonly share with family and friends. Again, at sweepstakes conventions you will likely hear people talking about giving away the precious prizes they won as gifts to their friends and family.

Non-winners or people who never enter sweepstakes think this "hobby" seems very peculiar. In fact, some people just can't understand sweeping and think it is all a waste of time and money. However, no one ever questions a golfer about the validity of hitting and chasing a little ball while trying to knock it into a hole. Nor does anyone think twice when someone says they are going to play tennis or go bowling. However, if you tell people that for fun you like entering sweepstakes you might be questioned. Why?

Some questions are easier to explain than others, but if you do venture to let others in on your little secret, just smile and remember not everyone is destined to be a winner like you.

Advanced Winning Secrets

It seems to be the norm that many people interested in this hobby often have a job or multiple jobs that requires them to work long hours. These same individuals may have additional responsibilities at home or elsewhere that must be fulfilled before attention can be given to their hobby, e.g. entering sweepstakes. Even retired individuals who enjoy this hobby are often found to be active and involved in many different projects. Regardless, a key element that everyone must master is time management. I know this was said before but the reality of life is that we all only operate with 24 hours in a day. However, we all know people who seem to get more done in less time than we do. What secret have they learned that we might have missed? Well, there is no real secret to it; rather it all has to do with priorities.

Only you can determine how much time and energy you are willing to put into this hobby. Yet, there is a truth that will always remain constant, and that is the more you focus your time and energy on one specific thing, the better you will become at that task.

Also, it is important that you create your own personal definition of "success." Don't fall into the trap of what others might say but determine for yourself a clearly defined goal or set of goals to achieve and set a time period when you want to accomplish this goal or goals.

You need to determine the amount of time and resources you can allocate for this hobby. Many successful sweepers have a certain time of day or night that they deem as "their sweepstakes time." A critical key to success is being able to balance both time and resources.

Do you have what it takes to be a winner? Not everyone does. *Real winners not only know what to do but when, and more importantly, if they need to act.* It is easy to think that in order for you to have the best chance of winning you must enter as many sweepstakes as possible in the shortest amount of time. In fact, you will read this countless times on the internet as well as read this in many publications from other authors. *Contrary to popular belief, not every sweepstakes is worth your time to enter.*

It is hard to resist the temptation when you see that long list of sweepstakes URLs. Your mind tells you that it will only take a second to click a few buttons to enter. We all have been brainwashed by the old saying: You can't win if you don't enter. Yes, that is true but you also need to know that not all sweepstakes, contests, lotteries or even raffles are equal, and you should be selective in what you enter.

Next know that the more steps or effort it takes to enter, the fewer the entries. This is great news for you. So, don't ignore sweepstakes that ask you to do that little extra before you are allowed to click and enter. Take that photograph and post it or write more than just a few words about why you like the product.

Another critical error so many in this hobby make is discounting how widely a specific sweepstakes is promoted and not just by the sponsor. Remember in this book we provided a list of over 100 websites that list sweepstakes. Think about that for a moment and the duplication that takes places. This is NOT a suggestion to ignore this valuable information. On the contrary, you should take advantage of this and enter the sweepstakes you find appealing that you honestly want to win. Realize that collectively there are millions of entries made to online sweepstakes every week! A little known truth that we previously disclosed is that some magazine sweepstakes offer large cash prizes multiple times in multiple magazines but only award one prize.

Again, let's stress that the reason for making these distinctions is not to suggest you should ignore these resources we have provided. No instead we think you should use this information mostly to chart your own course of action as well.

You don't necessarily have to "reinvent the wheel" to create success, but it doesn't hurt to try to improve how it rolls. This means you need to be creative. True success is not something that finds you but something you must actively seek.

Many people start locally--going to grocery and big box stores--not to shop but for the sole purpose of finding promotions. Also, watching your newspaper for store openings and looking everywhere for any promotion that may give away prizes.

Next, realize that most states understand the importance of tourism to their economy. Knowing such they often spend part of their advertising dollars using the same time tested method, namely sweepstakes promotions, that both large and small for-profit corporations use. Seek out the category of "travel sweepstakes" online. An extremely popular website many people find is VacationFun.com http://www.vacationfun.com/promo/sweepstakeslist.asp.

While this is a really fun site to enter to win various trips, a lot of people are entering on this specific website. Regardless, have fun and see this aspect of the hobby as an adventure versus a task you might dread.

As mentioned previously in this book, finding sweepstakes to enter is not going to be a problem but knowing exactly what to do next is the most critical. Make sure you study and understand the sweepstakes you are considering entering. You need to know the facts. What are the prizes being offered? What is the beginning and end time of when entries are accepted? How many entries are allowed? How many times can you enter?

Once you know the facts, then you need to determine if you really want to spend the time to enter. Next, you need to develop a systematic approach to enter sweepstakes and avoid at all costs any deviation from your strategy.

Winning comes to those who both *know* and *follow* the rules. This factor alone dictates a large part of your ability to win. While this seems common sense to almost everyone, this still is the biggest mistake most people make both in terms of beginners as well as those who are advanced and have been entering for years.

Let's be honest with ourselves, we all tend to get lazy. We like when someone else does the work for us, don't we? This may take the form of going online and clicking the provided link to enter without bothering to read the rules. This could mean getting a sweepstakes newsletter delivered to your email every week or month and not double checking the rules for accuracy before you start the process of entering to win.

Most of us don't read the rules because we feel like it is a waste of our time. But is it? It has been said by others in the past, and it is worth repeating again that the only time "success" comes before "work" is in the dictionary. If you live long enough you will realize that life has few shortcuts. So, if you want to achieve success then read the rules **before** you enter.

To summarize many of the key points again, understand that to be a consistent winner you *MUST* develop a systematic approach that takes into consideration the amount of time and resources you can allocate to this hobby. You need to set multiple goals you want to achieve for yourself with this hobby. Note that simply declaring that you want to be "a winner" is not descriptive enough but you must challenge yourself and answer the question: What will it really take for me to win? Notice I did not say, what is the specific "prize" you want to win? Focusing only on the prize means you are in some ways ignoring the process.

You need to take a moment now to jot down on a piece of paper at least three specific goals you want to achieve. Keep this list handy and update it when you need to but remain focused on these goals. Consider even posting these goals at your computer or whatever space you might use when you enter sweepstakes. Part of your success will be determined on how well you can stay focused on the goals you set for yourself. It is acceptable to have as a goal a certain prize but don't let that goal consume you either.

Now let's talk specifics about entries focusing for now on those that you enter online or by mail. You will find a section within the list of rules that specifically states the number of entries you are allowed per-day. Remember per-day means every 24 hours.

Below are various entry restrictions you commonly see spelled out when entering sweepstakes. Let's go step by step and discuss each entry restriction to make sure you understand what they truly mean.

One entry per household means only one person in your household can enter the sweepstakes. This also means that only one entry is allowed no matter how many different options that may be accepted, i.e. enter by online entry form, enter by text, enter by alternate means of entry etc. Unless otherwise stated in the rules, one entry means just that, one entry. If you on purpose or by mistake try to enter more than the official rules state, then you run the risk of being disqualified.

One entry per person. This is easy when you are talking about mailing in an entry but can prove to be more difficult when you are entering online. The reason is every computer that is connected to the internet has a specific "IP" or Internet Protocol address. The address itself consists of four sets of numbers with each set containing one to three digits with a single dot (.) separating each set of digits. An example might be: 89.135.4.207. These numbers represent your electronic address which allows you to send and receive information. These numbers do in fact provide information such as the continent, country and region as well as the city where the computer is located. Many sweepstakes sponsors capture this information in an effort to learn more about who is interested in their product or service. If you enter yourself and your spouse using the same computer, the sponsor may reject those entries because the rules states one entry per person and there is no way to verify that two different people actually entered separately. It might sound technical I know, but thousands upon thousands of entries are disqualified weekly for this violation.

One entry per email. As stated you are credited one entry for each email entered. Hypothetically you could enter using 200 different emails, but then you would have to check two hundred email boxes to see if any of them contained a winning notification. Who has time to check two hundred different email addresses?

One entry per person per email. Again each person can only enter one time and must use a separate email address.

One entry per day. Daily entry is usually defined from 12 a.m. to 11:59 p.m. You may want to consult with the official rules to see what is stated about timing.

One entry every 24 hours. If the promotion states that you can only enter every 24 hours, then you need to note the time when you last entered. If you entered one day at 8:00 a.m. then you must enter the next day, no earlier than 8:00 a.m.

One entry per-week. You can only enter once every seven days.

One entry per-month. You can only enter once per calendar month.

One entry per quarter. You can enter once every three months.

Specified number of entries. The sponsor only allows a certain number of entries.

Unlimited entries. You can enter as many entries as you want.

Since we are clear as to the number of entries that are allowed, let's now talk about which sweepstakes is the best one to enter. Unfortunately, it is not that simple. Choosing what sweepstakes you want to enter is much like choosing the flavor of ice cream you want to eat. You need to look at the prizes offered first to see if you want to win those prizes. Second, you need to read the rules to make sure you are qualified to enter. If you truly want to win the prize, you need to max out the number of entries you can enter.

Often people feel conflicted because they find more than one sweepstakes they really want to enter.

So, let's pose a hypothetical question. Let's say we can only afford to mail in a total of three entries and this sweepstakes only receives a total of 50 entries. Would it be better to enter one sweepstakes three times or three different sweepstakes one time?

"In the first case, you have three entries out of 50, so your chance of winning assuming all drawings have equal chance of being picked is $3/50 = 0.06$.

If you enter three contests one time, assuming each contest is the same, then your chance of winning at least one of them is the complement to losing all of them. This probability is given by $1-(49/50)3 = 73511/25000 = 0.058808$.

So it seems you have a slightly better chance of winning at least once if put all three of your bets in one contest."

Source: http://math.stackexchange.com/questions/24281/odds-of-winning-a-contest

In reading this book, it should be obvious by now that finding sweepstakes to enter will not be a problem, but finding the time and energy and resources to enter as many as you want will prove more difficult.

The system you develop must be your own. Don't be overly influenced by others who might be successful claiming they have the solution, but that does not necessarily mean what they do will work for you.

Another important distinction that needs to be pointed out is that "entering sweepstakes" today has taken on a whole new meaning. Many people focus only online because it is cheaper and easier. Others swear by doing mail-in sweepstakes. Still others will tell you that they win more entering using Twitter™ or by texting to win than other methods. Regardless, while entering sweepstakes for most is a fun hobby, there is work involved.

What Really Happens With My Information

The truth of the matter is that many companies running prize promotions as well as those who include a warranty card in with a product you purchase are in fact collecting information. Some companies use your information in hopes of establishing a direct marketing relationship with their consumer, and yes, some companies do sell your information to other advertisers that may or may not be affiliated with their company. However, most companies have found that sweepstakes names are not worth the cost of keypunching.

If there is a negative aspect of entering sweepstakes, it is the uncomfortable feeling many people have with the amount of information you are asked to disclose. Sweepstakes sponsors are keenly aware that the more information they ask, the less inclined people are to share and enter. There is a fine line where most sponsors seek to create a balance.

A question that many people might be curious about is why corporations ask for your date of birth? If the sweepstakes involves a company that sells tobacco or alcohol, this might be obvious because consumption of either products is illegal for minors. However, one specific concern corporations have when placing a sweepstakes online is making sure they are in compliance with The Child Online Privacy Protection Act or "COPPA" for short. This federal set of rules was put in place to protect the privacy information of children younger than 13 who may be submitting information to a website. Specifically, the Federal Trade Commission acts as the lead agency that determines if the website is directed at children. Further they consider several factors such as the subject matter of the site itself and the visual and/or audio content. The language used as well as any advertising that is specifically directed towards children including the age of any model used or if animated characters or other child-oriented features are displayed is all evaluated. Parental notice and consent are requirements whenever a child's personal information is collected.

A person's date of birth also gives the sponsor knowledge of the age of the individual viewing their website. Knowing the age of the individual will give clues as to what messages or advertising might be appealing to this group.

Realistically when you enter sweepstakes, you should expect to see more promotional mail in your virtual mailbox and less likely (but possibly) your postal mailbox.

Why Do Sweepstakes Ask for My Phone Number and Email?

In some cases the sponsor or prize provider simply wants an easy method to contact you in case you are the winner. However, if you find that providing your phone number is a conditional requirement in order to enter into a sweepstakes, then you will likely be asked to agree to receive telemarketing calls about sponsor's goods or services. The underlying purpose of this is an attempt to establish a business relationship with the entrant which in turn exempts them from having to abide by the do-not-call lists. This is a gray area at best because at the present time neither the Federal Trade Commission nor the Federal Communication Commission have made an official ruling on this interpretation.

Many avid sweepstakes professionals use a separate phone number so not to be bothered by sales calls on their home phone number. It is a good idea to also establish a separate email account specifically for your sweepstakes entries. Make this email as generic as possible and not create an email that gives any impression that it is for sweepstakes only. Many people establish a secondary Facebook™ account as well, however, Facebook™ frowns on this practice.

Any additional emails received from sponsors after you enter a sweepstakes are required by law to comply with the Controlling the Assault of Non-Solicited Pornography and Marketing Act of 2003 also known as the CAN-SPAM Act. This Act regulates commercial messages that are considered to be advertising and/or promotional for a product or service. This Act requires the sender of the message to have a functioning email address or some other internet based mechanism that allows the recipient of the message to request removal from the sender's list to avoid getting further communications from the sender.

If you start getting emails right after entering the sweepstakes, it is advisable to wait until after the promotion is over before choosing to unsubscribe. While the law is clear that an individual is not required to subscribe and receive promotional material, it is better to be safe and continue to receive the information at least for a limited time.

You should always give an actual physical mailing address and not rely on a post office box. Many sweepstakes do not accept the use of a post office box for your official address.

Obviously, sponsors of the sweepstakes would prefer that you are an actual consumer that uses and buys their product or service, but they can't demand that of you in order to qualify.

It is not uncommon to see sweepstakes where companies place a crack-n-peel sticker on their packaging that will contain a code. In most cases you will need to go to the sponsor's website and register before entering the code. In this case of prize promotion it is easy to see how the company makes money because you are in fact buying the product. But again an alternate method of entry (AMOE) will be provided.

The point of the promotion is to incentivize consumers that may not already be a buyer of the product. If the consumer sees displayed on the package a promotion offering a chance for free trip or a cash prize, they in turn may be swayed to buy or try the product. Companies also view promotions as part of their new customer acquisition cost by seeking to influence your behavior and get you into the habit of buying their product on a regular basis.

Sponsor Appreciation

Many people rightly wonder why companies and/or individuals offer sweepstakes prizes. What are their motives? For some it is as simple as hoping to create a buzz or perhaps to generate web traffic. For others, sweepstakes are used to help with the introduction of a new product or service. In short, sponsors of sweepstakes want to increase their business presence with a hope of also increasing sales of their product or service.

Some sweepstakes sponsors in the past have had high hopes of getting a good targeted mailing lists of individuals who are interested in using their products only to find that the names, addresses and emails they received from people who entered to win the denture cream, cat food, dog food, diapers or baby formula are actually people who don't have dentures, a cat, dog or baby. Folks who enjoy entering sweepstakes for fun and possibly for a little profit have made it more difficult for sponsors. Regardless, this method of promotion still works for some advertisers and therefore will continue to be used.

Responsible sweepers need to do their part in being reasonable and showing a little restraint when entering sweepstakes. Also, show the common courtesy of sending a note of appreciation when you win a prize of any significant value. The bottom line is a little gratitude goes a long way. Unfortunately, as with many things, there are a few people who just don't get it.

Not that long ago at a national sweepstakes convention this topic was addressed by one of the speakers. It was shocking that a few of the attendees actually challenged the speaker acting as if winning prizes was more of an absolute right versus a privilege. Granted, the rules don't require a purchase or for you to even like or use the product; yet there should be a common courtesy extended to everyone.

One of the worst things anyone who enters sweepstakes can do is not be respectful of the sponsor. Bragging to the sponsor about how you just enter sweepstakes and have never used their product or service serves no purpose. Also, arriving at a sponsor's event wearing a tee shirt that is promoting another brand; and, yes, this has happened, basically is destroying the hobby that you claim to enjoy.

Pitfalls Sponsors Face

If you enter sweepstakes on a regular basis, then you know that sponsors cannot make you purchase a product or service as a qualifier for entering a sweepstakes. The payment of monies under the law is what is known as "consideration." You are also aware that all legitimately run sweepstakes must have a free alternative method of entry (AMOE). However, many sponsors do not realize that the act of consideration goes beyond just the payment of monies but extends further. Note that simple tasks like filling out 3"x 5" cards or watching television to find an answer or listening to the radio or calling a toll free number are not thought to be "consideration."

Passing the threshold of consideration takes place when an entrant is required to make substantial effort, and time to participate in the promotion. If the entrant is required to fill out long questionnaires or required to make multiple trips to a store, then this is consideration. Likewise, requiring you to refer a friend may in some states also be considered consideration. Receiving a commercial benefit from the entrant also constitutes consideration. Many states define the act of consideration differently so it can and often is confusing to sponsors. Florida, for instance, has the view that consideration "need not involve money or anything of monetary value." Rather it "may consist of a benefit to the promisor, or a detriment to the promisor," or if the promise "does anything which he is not bound to do, or refrains from doing anything which he has the right to do."

As technology changes and the delivery methods of promotions change the question of what constitutes consideration on the part of the entrant will be ever expanding. Change is one constant that not only affects life in general but the world of sweepstakes as well.

Another pitfall many sponsors can and often face is their treatment of entries. Regardless of the method of entry all entries must be treated alike. You cannot give better odds or more entries to an individual that may have purchased your product or services versus another who mailed in an alternative means of entry. Another line inadvertently crossed is when the promotion is crafted whereby the sponsor's actions favor the purchase based entry over the non-purchase entry. An example of this is when a sweepstakes print ad listed four ways to enter the sweepstakes but the prominent ad copy displayed "Buy X Brand." In tiny print at the bottom of the ad was an alternative means of entry method. This was deemed a violation and an enforcement action was taken against the company by state regulators.

Promotional Management Companies and Judging Agencies

Most companies of any size who plan on implementing sweepstakes promotions and/or contests realize the complexity of the laws surrounding this endeavor. Because of the liability factor alone most understand this is beyond their marketing team's expertise so they seek out the professional advice of a promotional management company. Most of these companies will offer services that include all aspects of the creation of the promotion. Most focus on making sure that each aspect of the promotion is both legal and administered properly.

Unfortunately, for people entering sweepstakes they may find that promotional management companies and/or judging agencies tend to have a secretive side and have a reputation of being less than helpful. There is a reason for this standoffish attitude. Below explains why you may find it difficult to get the answer or answers you are seeking.

Judging Agency - Policy and Procedures

Almost all agencies have a written policy that states: "Nobody in the company, yes that means nobody, may answer consumer questions about prize promotions *in progress*. If someone calls with a question (no matter how innocuous sounding), please keep the following wording by your phone, and USE IT WORD FOR WORD.

"Thank you for calling XYZ Agency, so that no individual has an unfair advantage over any other individual we cannot answer questions about a sweepstakes (contest) in progress. If you have any questions or concerns we suggest you read the rules. Invariably a careful reading of the rules will give you the answer you are looking for."

This is time for the "broken record" technique. Just keep repeating that exact phrase over and over if they continue to press. Not only could your response be unfair to some entrants, but it may be subject to misunderstanding and come back to haunt the company.

IMPORTANT: Certain clients, notably health and beauty aid companies, have hired so-called mystery shoppers to call in and record the agency's answer. Any exception to the above response could result in not only legal problems but the loss of a client.

THERE IS NO EXCEPTION TO THIS RULE. In the past we have been told hired agencies have called with the following inquiries...

"In the X sweepstakes my Mother is sick; if she wins can she have the cash or can I donate the trip?"

"I just have this one tiny quick question ... "

"The rules say 3x5 paper can I enter a 3x5 index card?"

"I see someone at your company wrote a book. If I buy it, do I have better chance to win in X sweepstakes."

No matter the question. REMEMBER, NO EXCEPTIONS means NO EXCEPTIONS no matter how simple the question may sound.

If an individual calls about a sweepstakes that just closed, if they are a winner calling about the prize direct the call to "prize fulfillment (extension X)." If they want a winners list suggest they see the rules for instructions. If they want to know when prizes are picked, prizes shipped, etc. tell them to send a self-addressed stamped envelope to the appropriate company address. Other than winners...no questions can be answered on the phone. "Being helpful" could (and has) caused MAJOR problems.

If a client is calling with a question transfer that call to the account executive on that business. If that person is not at his/her desk, transfer the calls to a Vice President or above only.

Knowing that it might be difficult to get answers, some people will still want to try or might have other reasons for wanting to contact a judging agency. Realizing this might be the case you will find several resource links below:

The Contest Queens List of Promotional Management Companies & Judging Agencies
http://contestqueen.com/us-resources/run-a-sweepstakes/promotional-management-companies-judging-agencies/

Sweeties Sweeps List of Sweepstakes Judging Agencies and Administrators
http://sweetiessweeps.com/2009/01/sweepstakes-judging-agencies-and-administrators.html

Judging Agency Litigation

The section below is a recap of an experience Jeffrey Feinman, the founder and former CEO/President of Ventura Associates, faced while managing the day to day operations.

Defectum humoris non curat lex ('the law does not reward humorlessness')

There are days that I think I should have listened to my father and become a doctor (LOL). Seriously, I will say at times I thought that the major joy of this business was taking home my paycheck. Of course, friends would often say, "Are you kidding it must be great to hand somebody a check for $100,000 and see the joy in their face." Sadly, more often than not, sweepstakes only brought out all the bad things that are linked to greed and avarice.

I remember speaking at a seminar and a young woman came up to me after my speech and said, "I am just curious, I understand the reason for most rules, but why you would have a rule like the following." She then thrust a magazine ad into my hand and she had carefully highlighted the following rule...

"Rule 16. Release: By receipt of any prize, winners agree (and agree to confirm in writing, if so requested) to release and hold harmless Advertiser, advertising agency, independent judging organization, and any promotional partners, each of their parent, subsidiary, affiliate and related companies, and each of its and their respective officers, directors, employees and agents (collectively the "Released Parties") from and against any losses, damages, rights, claim or cause of action of any kind arising, in whole or in part, directly or indirectly, out of participation in the Promotion or resulting directly or indirectly from acceptance, possession, use or misuse of any prize awarded in connection with the Promotion including any travel related thereto or any events during such travel, including without limitation personal injury, death and/ or property damage, as well as claims based on publicity rights, defamation and/or invasion of privacy."

She said, "I understand how you would have litigation if you are trying to collect money from folks. But why would have a problem when you are giving folks money?" She then smiled and said, "Surely, you have never been sued."

The answer is I have been sued so many times I doubt there is a single state that doesn't have the record of some action taken against us. The good news is we have won all these suits. However, the bad news is you can win a lawsuit in court and still wind up with a bill from a law firm for $50,000.

In answer to the question why we need rule 16 here is an actual case.

California. We were the judging organization on "The Race to Beauty" sweepstakes for a major cosmetics company. The grand prize winner, of a new Chevrolet and $25,000 in cash, was a young man from Los Angeles. About six months after he received the car he was in a major automotive crash on a California freeway. The way we learned this fact was that a process server showed at our office. We (as the judging organization), the advertising agency that had created the ad, and the cosmetic company were all named in a $1,500,000.00 lawsuit. The basis of his case was that this auto accident was so severe he would be out of work for as long as a year. In addition he had substantial medical bills and significant pain and suffering. He asked that we were all jointly liable for these damages. Why was he suing us? His logic was that had he not won the sweepstakes, and had we not given him the prize he never would have been in the accident.

I was hard pressed to believe their lawyer was so stupid that he would accept such a case. As it turned out the sweepstakes winner and the plaintiff had finished law school the previous year. He had not been able to find a job as a lawyer. In preliminary discussions with him we quickly determined that after his accident he had a brainstorm. That was, if he brought the lawsuit himself, he hoped we would each pay him $50,000 plus for the nuisance value. That is, he knew he couldn't win. He knew we knew he couldn't win. But his assumption was (a) it would cost each of us $25,000 plus to retain out of state attorneys (b) we would have to spend time and energy dealing with his frivolous lawsuit (c) we wouldn't want adverse publicity.

He was partially right. Our client's lawyers said, "Rather than waste time and money on this why don't we each pay him a few thousand dollars to go away." I said I would rather spend $100,000 in legal fees than give this guy even $500. First of all, I was not going to be blackmailed. Secondly, this guy would tell his friends and all it would do is encourage more frivolous lawsuits from other sweepstakes winners.

As it turned out our attorney had an even better idea. He suggested we ask the court to impose Rule 11 sanctions. Rule 11 requires an attorney to make an objectively reasonable inquiry into the facts and law prior to filing a lawsuit and not to pursue an action that is not objectively reasonable based on the facts. A lawyer found guilty of Rule 11 could have significant fine levied against him.

Obviously, this young man was not aware of Rule 11. Perhaps one example of his lack of legal knowledge. Perhaps one of the many reasons he had not found a job after graduating. In addition, of course, was that his loss of income was hard for him to pursue given he was out of work.

In the final analysis he collected nothing and had significant costs. However, my point is that our pain and suffering was perhaps greater than his.

In short, it's been said that sweepstakes brings out the greed in folks. One fellow remarked that there is a touch of all of the seven deadly sins (pride, greed, lust, envy, gluttony, wrath, and sloth) irrevocably linked to the prize promotion industry!

What Happens After You Win?

It is worth noting that if you are a winner of a prize generally valued at $600 or more, then you will likely be asked to sign an affidavit that states your contact information and spells out the rules of the promotion.

All legitimate affidavits will require a signature of the winner whereby agreeing that you have not only abided by the rules, but that you are not affiliated in any way with the company that is running the promotion. Some affidavits will also require that your signature be witnessed by someone else and many times by an official notary. If the prize allows for a guest then the guest may also be asked to sign a release form. You may be required to fill out an affidavit for prize amount lower than the stated $600 and in one instance an affidavit was even required for a tee-shirt. Thankfully, those occasions are rare because doing so is unwarranted and cost prohibitive for the sponsor.

Back in the early days of sweepstakes if you were the winner of a big prize you were not only required to sign an affidavit, but you might be visited by a private detective agency. That's right, certain companies, mainly tobacco companies were, known to hire private detectives to do a little snooping asking neighbors and maybe at your place of employment if you were an actual smoker. The winner of their sweepstakes promotions generally were required to be smokers, and they wanted to insure that people entering the sweepstakes were telling the truth before the prize was awarded.

Today, background checks performed by qualified private investigators are still used sparingly but not widely publicized. The promotion and type of prize or prizes offered generally dictate the level of scrutiny that is warranted. Examples of when an investigation might be performed is if the entrant is going to receive a large check or if money is being spent to promote the winner of the promotion.

Another example of when an investigation may be necessary is when the winner is meeting a famous individual or will be involved with a center court or on field presentation. The last thing any judging agency wants to happen is for the sponsor to be embarrassed or receive bad publicity.

What to do about taxes?

Most people are aware that if the value of the prize or service received by the prize provider and or sweepstakes sponsor is $600 or more, then the winner will receive an IRS Form 1099 Misc. that must be used when filing income taxes. However, there is a common myth among those in the sweepstakes world that needs to be dispelled. Even if the amount awarded is less than $600 and you do not receive any form, you are still required to report ALL your winnings to the IRS.

One of the most common complaints of big winners is that they have to pay such high taxes on their prizes. Unfortunately, there is no legal method to avoid paying such a high price. Know that the government keeps a close watch over lotteries, sweepstakes, and contests to make sure winners are paying the taxes due. If you fail to report your winnings, you'll likely get caught and you will also likely owe an additional fine. It's best to keep everything on the up and up from the very start.

But how can you get away with paying the least taxes?

It is recommended that you consult a tax lawyer or an agent from your local Internal Revenue Office.

Usually it's done this way.

If the prize is a cash prize, of course, you must declare the entire sum of money and deduct expenses incurred in winning.

If the cash prize is merchandise, you declare the fair market value of the prize and, again, deduct the expenses incurred in winning.

One little warning: You are never allowed to declare any losses. What does this mean? If you win a couch you're ahead of the game no matter what. If the retail value is $1,000 and you sell it for $50 you can't declare the so-called loss of $950. This all has to do with fair market value, so pay close attention to what follows.

What is the fair market value? The definition of the fair market value is the amount a willing seller, not forced to sell, will demand, and a willing buyer, not forced to buy, will pay.

In other words, let's say you win a car worth $10,000. You cannot sell the car to your brother for $5,000 and declare this amount as the value of the prize on your tax forms. Many people are confused about this very point. Chances are you could sell the car for an amount pretty close to its so-called retail value, so you'll probably end up having to declare something close to the retail value on your tax forms.

Suppose you win a custom-made couch, made to order for your living room and it comes in bright red only, because you listed your living room colors on your entry form. In this case, the value of the couch has a great deal to do with its measurements and color, and since it was made to order, it probably has a greater value to you than any prospective buyer. But suppose you decide that you don't want the couch after you win it, and you want to sell it. Selling the couch depends on your finding a willing buyer whose living room is close to the same size as yours, and whose color scheme is the same. It's something like trying to sell a piece of used furniture, and there's nothing you can do about the size and color.

Now suppose there's only one prospective buyer in your community. If this is the case, you can't honestly insist that your $1,000 couch is in great demand. You will probably have to sell it for pretty much what the buyer is willing to pay. You may try to bargain with him, but he might just walk out the door. You're stuck with a big, red couch that you don't want.

In such a case, the fair market value will be substantially less than the retail value. It may actually turn out to be the wholesale value. It may even be less than this.

In many cases, the value of the merchandise is inflated by the sponsors of the sweepstakes/contest. Naturally, they want to make their gift look as important to the contestants as possible. This inflated value is not the amount that you must put on your tax returns.

People believe that the amount you must pay taxes on is the retail value, the wholesale value, or the amount you get when you sell. None of these values are necessarily correct. What you must pay tax on the amount a bona fide buyer would pay if he or she bought the merchandise.

The only instances in which you can declare substantially less than the value of the item are cases where the item is custom-made, or so unique that you can't find a buyer. The couch mentioned earlier is a good example of this. Or suppose you win a mink bathing suit by a high fashion designer.

Even if you decide to keep the item, you need only declare the fair market value. That is, the couch, the mink bathing suit, or any other such hard-to-sell item need not be declared at full value, even if you're a willing receiver.

This means you have to determine what the fair market value is.

This is not especially easy. Check prices in newspapers, magazines, mail-order catalogs, direct-mail advertisements, and online. These prices will probably not differ much. You certainly will have to research the matter very carefully.

Do you always have to pay taxes? Sometimes you may be the lucky winner of a sweepstakes/contest in which the sponsor offers to pay your taxes for you. If this is the case, you must list this reimbursement on your tax forms as another source of income, and you'll end up paying taxes on the taxes!

There are have been instances involving companies located outside the United States that offer the promotion and they fail to send the winner a 1099-M Form. Regardless, the IRS expects you to pay taxes on your winnings.

What are deductible expenses? First of all, you can only deduct these expenses if you win. Suppose you enter a thousand sweepstakes and win nothing, none of these items can be deducted on your tax returns. You must be a winner. In other words, your sweepstakes hobby must provide you with a source of income.

Here are some of the items you can deduct if you do win.

1. The money you spend on stamps.
2. The money you spend on paper, pens, index cards, stickers, address labels, pads of paper, scrap paper, paper clips, staples, dictionaries, and that big calendar you purchased so you could keep track of closing dates.
3. The price of any sweepstakes books you purchase.
4. The price of the subscriptions to any online sweepstakes newsletters.
5. If you should happen to win a lottery, you may deduct the price of all your losing tickets.

The IRS announced on January 30, 1973, that winners of state lotteries are eligible to deduct the cost of losing tickets against their winnings when they are listing deductions on their tax forms.

Of course, as in all other cases, this gambling loss can only be claimed if you win something!

Reality Sweepstakes TV – Believe It or Not It is Been Done

Can a person live off nothing but things they win from contests? Well, just when you thought life could not get any weirder we need to finally expose this true story to the sweepers in America about the 1998 Japanese Nippon Televison hit show sensation involving a man whose stage name was Nasubi.

The following is an account of the TV show that lasted over a YEAR in Japan.

NASUBI

"Nippon Television's (NTV) producers have obviously never heard of the Geneva Convention. If they had, they wouldn't have treated poor Nasubi the way they did. They wouldn't have stripped him naked and shut him in an apartment, alone with no food, furniture, household goods, or entertainment. They wouldn't have kept him there for over a year until he had won $10, 000 in prizes by sending in postcards to contests. They wouldn't have cut him off from the world and they would have told him that he was on nation-wide TV.

It all started one snowy day in January, 1998 with an audition. The audition consisted of choosing lots because the only talent needed for this challenge was luck. A group of aspiring comedians showed up, and among them was a young man whose stage name is Nasubi, which means eggplant. Nasubi was 'lucky' that day, and was chosen over other aspiring young comedians for a mysterious "show-business related job." He was immediately blindfolded and driven to a tiny one room apartment somewhere in Tokyo.

When he arrived at the apartment, he was shown a stand full of magazines, a huge pile of postcards, and told to strip naked. The room was empty except for a cushion, a table, a small radio, a telephone, some notebooks, and a few pens. There was not a crumb of food, a square of toilet paper, or any form of entertainment. Whatever he needed, he was to win by sending thousands of postcards into contests. The producers left and Nasubi was on his own in his unique survival challenge. Imagine what was going through his mind: How am I going to eat? Why are they doing this to me? How long will it take to get out of here? He must have thought he was in a bad episode of The Prisoner.

He got some jelly, a 1,560 yen value, leaving him with 998,440 yen left to win. That day, he ate food for the first time in two weeks! On February 22nd, he won a 5-kg bag of rice. Unfortunately, he had no cooking utensils. At first, he tried eating it raw, but eventually devised a cooking method where he put it in an empty can beside a burner for an hour until it was 'cooked.' He ate about a half cup of rice a day using two pens for chopsticks.

Life was tough for Nasubi--he was obviously lonely, uncomfortable and bored but he seemed to be continually cheerful in the face of adversity. Putting on a bold face when one is suffering is one of the most admired traits in Japan and this was a big reason for the program's incredible popularity. He spent his days writing postcards, and sent out between 3,000 and 8,000 a month! It must have been incredibly discouraging because by the end of March, he had only won 66,840 yen, leaving him with 933,160 yen left to win.

Every time Nasubi won a contest, he did a victory dance and made up a strange song about the prize he had won and how happy he was. You've never seen anyone's face light up the way Nasubi's did when he heard a knock at the door or the telephone rang. In this picture, we see him celebrating after he won a poster of his favorite TV star, an attractive young woman named Ryoko Hirose. His apartment was gradually filling up and he was beginning to live something resembling a human life. Of course, there were some bad moments too, especially the day he won a TV but realized his apartment had no antennae or cable!

A doctor's visit in May, after five months in the room, revealed Nasubi to be in perfect health! No scurvy, no fleas or lice, and no signs of malnutrition. He had lost a lot of weight, and his ribs were showing through his skin, but his blood tests and a physical examination revealed no other problems. His fingernails had grown to several inches long and his hair and beard were getting rather unmanageable by that time, but they were annoyances rather than dangers. It is incredible what the human body can survive and how resilient people are. Who would have thought that it was possible to live like that?

Near the end of May, Nasubi's rice ran out, and he was reduced to eating dog food. It was heart wrenching seeing him pray every night for rice.

By June, the show had become incredibly popular and the mass media had found out where Nasubi was staying. In the middle of the night, he was awakened by a producer with a flashlight, blindfolded and moved to a new apartment. He was told that it was to "change his luck" but the real reason was that the producers were worried he would find out that the entire nation was watching him. Unfortunately, the people who moved his things to the new apartment forgot to bring his rice! One of the few times we got to see Nasubi really angry was when he said, "How could you forget my rice??? How could you? Don't you know how important my rice is?" He seemed to be on the point of breaking.

By the end of June, his total had reached 550,000 yen, halfway to his goal of one million yen!

In July, a live internet feed to Nasubi's room was set up. Because he was nude, they needed a staff of 50 to maintain the site and control the ever-present dot over Nasubi's private parts. Until this time, some people had thought the whole thing was fake, but the live internet feed convinced everyone that the show was not being staged. The site was incredibly popular and received thousands of hits every day. Part of the reason the show and live internet feed were so popular was because he played with everything he won. He often talked to a stuffed animal that he won and named Venus, or rolled around on the set car tires.

August and September were some of the toughest months. He went for two weeks in August without winning a single contest, and most of the things he won in September had almost no value and he advanced only about 10,000 yen that month. One happy moment in September was his 'Summer Holiday' at the beach (naked of course). It was felt that having spent eight months in the apartment, he needed to get out. In October he moved again.

When he won a video deck to go with his TV, he was able to watch his two videos--an exercise video and a cycling tape. He saw a woman for the first time in 10 months. In November, he won two rolls of toilet paper, a huge moment in his life! He also won a Sony Play Station, which went well with the train driving game, and special controller he had won earlier and he spent hours in front of the TV. He spent about three days playing with it and then decided that he was wasting too much time playing with it.

Nasubi's first ordeal ended in December. The thing that put him over the top was, of course, a bag of rice. Unfortunately, he didn't know that he had won and continued writing postcards. That night, he was paid another visit by the producer, who crept in with Christmas crackers to wake him up in the middle of the night. There was nothing congratulatory in the producer's manner as he refused to answer Nasubi's questions, and continued setting off the Christmas Cracker's until Nasubi realized that he had successfully completed his challenge. Nasubi was curled up into a fetal position, and seemed unused to talking to other people.

Finally, he was given back his clothes, and for the first time in a year, he knew what it was like to wear clothes other than women's underwear. They gave him a bowl of ramen, and let him out on the street. They also took him to an amusement park and to Korea to eat his favorite food, Korean barbecue. After his 'rest' was over, he found himself back in a room, all alone again, but this time in Korea, a country whose language he could neither speak nor write! This time however, his goal was to earn his airfare home. It was about $400 US.

He won the required money by getting a TV, expensive food and other prizes relatively quickly, so the staff made his challenge more and more difficult (without telling him) and decided that he would have to get a business class and then a first-class ticket. Nasubi began to become suspicious that Nasubi must have achieved his goal so the producer paid him another visit. He was finally flown back to Japan.

This time, they took him into a Television studio, and led him in a box that he thought was a room. Out of habit, he took off his clothes and waited. Suddenly, the walls of the 'room' fell down and the 'ceiling' was raised. He found himself naked in front of a thousand cheering fans and the hosts of Denpa Shonen came out and explained everything that had been happening over the last year and three months to him.

He was told that his diary had become a number one best seller grossing hundreds of thousands of yen, that when he ate the bowl of Ramen at the end of his ordeal in Japan the footage had been used in an immensely popular TV commercial, and that his website had grossed huge amounts of money.

Some things that Nasubi won during his year and three months of 'Living off contests':

2 vacuums, rice (4 times, 35 kg), shoes, a watermelon, a cutlery set, ice cream, chocolates, natto (twice), bicycle, television (no antennae in the apartment), a globe, stuffed animals, dental care products, videos, pickled eggplant, a poster of Hirose Ryoko, free tickets to the Spice Girls movie, a coupon for a free English lesson (twice), headphones, a CD Rom, videos, a huge box of potato chips, duck meat, a barbecue, several unidentifiable varieties of

Japanese snacks, a belt, some sexy women's underwear (which he tried to wear but couldn't put on), Matsutake mushrooms, steak, a tent, an attaché case, a set of tires, a photo book, golf balls.

Some things that Nasubi never won during his year and three months of 'Living off contests' clothes, plates, soap, books, a bed or futon, sheets and blankets, pots or pans.

So, what was the point of the Nasubi experiment? Ostensibly, it was to test the thesis that contests had become so ubiquitous that it would be possible to live entirely on what one had won in them. This was called kensho seikatsu (Living off contests).

Of course, the real reason is that programs involving human suffering are extremely popular in Japan. The gambaru genre, started in the 1980's with the immensely popular show Za Gaman, a show in which university students competed in contests to see who could stand the most pain, eat the most unpleasant foods, and perform the most humiliating tasks. Denpa Shonen is a logical continuation of this trend, and the stunts are becoming more and more dangerous/appalling.

Someday a Japanese comedian is going to die in a horrible accident and this sort of program will be immediately pulled from the airwaves. People are travelling through dangerous countries, fighting bulls without any training, scaring the life out of innocent victims and playing incredibly cruel practical jokes. It's inevitable that a tragic accident will happen. There will be condemnations and recriminations, and people will say that they never liked them, knew they were dangerous, and definitely never watched them. But almost everybody is watching them because they are fascinating.

First of all, they are hilarious. Even people who hate the idea of them usually can't help laughing if they watch them. You also sympathize with the comedians and feel sorry for them because they seem to be victims of the evil TV producers or their circumstances, but never think about how you, the viewer who is increasing the show's ratings are actually responsible. The shows are funny, and in a strange way, educational too. A lot of people learned about what humans are and are not capable of by watching Nasubi. People like to be shocked, they get addicted by the suspense, and they love rooting for the suffering individual when they get close to achieving their goal.

If you want to see Nasubi for yourself, go to your local video store (in Japan) and it will be in the comedy section."

Winning Stories - Three Prize Wins of John Minges

Prize Win #1

Winning a Car! A few years ago I was made aware of a raffle that was taking place to benefit our local homeless shelter. I had served on the board of directors and also as president of the organization many years ago. The shelter was in the process of building a new building and raising money through a fundraising raffle. Tickets were only ten dollars each, which was way too low, and they were giving away a brand new 2015 Mazda. I previously planned on making a contribution to the building campaign so instead I decided to buy tickets. This proved to be a great decision. My ticket was drawn, and I was declared the winner! This was perfect timing because my nephew was turning 16 soon. Now I'm on the hunt for another raffle or sweepstakes that has a car or truck as a prize because my nephew has a younger brother who is now 14. Fortunately, I have a few years before I have to win the next one. Wish me luck.

Prize Win #2

As part of learning and experiencing any hobby, you will make many mistakes along the way, even in winning. Below is one example of a mistake I made.

The prize was a dinner where 50 people would attend to see a former unnamed sports celebrity. The prize was valued at $500. However, the event was taking place in New York, and I live North Carolina. Where I originally saw the sweepstakes listed I was in a rush that day and while I am embarrassed to say this, I did not read the rules but just quickly entered the sweepstakes and quickly forgot about it. Upon receiving an email stating that I had won, I read the rules listed below.

The prize conditions stated the following:

"All travel related expenses including but not limited to airfare, hotel accommodations, ground transportation to and from home, taxes, gratuities, incidentals, upgrades, insurance, service charges, airport surcharges, luggage fees, departure taxes, hotel/resort or property fees, food & beverage and personal expenses such as telephone/Internet charges, and gift shop purchases are the sole responsibility of prize winner.

All expenses related to the acceptance or use of the prize is the sole responsibility of prize winner.

In the event any prize winner or his/her guest engages in behavior that, as determined by the Sponsor and in its sole discretion, is obnoxious or threatening, illegal, or that is intended to annoy, abuse, threaten or harass any other person, the Sponsor reserves the right to eject from or deny admission to prize event for such person, with no further compensation.

If a prize notification or prize is returned as undeliverable, or if winner is found to be ineligible or not in compliance with these rules, that winner will be disqualified, and the prize may be awarded to an alternate winner in a separate random drawing.

Prizes are not redeemable for cash. Prizes are non-assignable or transferable. No substitution is permitted except if the prize is unavailable, in which case a prize of equal or greater value will be awarded. No cash in lieu of prizes and no exchange or substitution of prizes, except at the sole discretion of the Sponsor. Any other incidental expenses on prize not specified herein are the winner's sole responsibility."

With all that said, I politely declined the prize because it did not make sense for me to spend all that money to go to an event that honestly I really didn't want to go to anyway. In short, the moral of this story is make sure you really want to win before you enter not after you are notified!

Prize Win #3

Recently, I was fortunate enough to win a vacation package worth $4,450; I'll tell you more about how that happened in a moment. The vacation package included hotel rooms for up to four guests as well as airfare and a hundred dollars in gift cards for incidentals. I was notified of the win and after filling out the affidavit, verified and approved I was officially declared the winner. I was then contacted by a travel agent to handle the details. The vacation location was in driving distance, for my wife and me; we invited another couple to join us who happen to live on the other side of the country. While the airfare was for four people in coach, I was able to negotiate with the travel agent to buy just two first class tickets for the other couple instead of four coach tickets.

The sweepstakes was actually an on-package promotion where you would buy the product and peel off a sticker and enter the code. The product cost to purchase the package was a dollar. As with all sweepstakes, there was a no purchase option whereby you could mail in a self-addressed stamped envelope to receive a prize code. Beyond the main grand prize, there were three other prizes that were not very exciting. Each of the other prizes also were worth less than fifty dollars in retail value. I knew in the beginning it was a long shot but took the chance anyway. Of course there was no way to accurately know exactly the odds because the biggest unknown variable was how many people would in fact buy the product and take the time to enter the code or how many would mail and get a code. Another variable that was buried in the rules was that only so many codes could be entered in one day. Even though I read the rules several times, I first missed this important fact and made the mistake of entering too many codes. Fortunately, I later caught my mistake, but I know some of my entries were probably disqualified for several days. So again the moral of this story is not to give up and read the rules over and over.

I believe that if I remain persistent and optimistic that I will continue to win prizes both big and small for the rest of my life.

Sweepstakes Acronyms

#10 - This is a business-sized envelope that measuring
4 $\frac{1}{8}$ x 9 $\frac{1}{2}$

Addy, Addie - your physical home address

AFFY - Affidavit - The official paperwork you need to sign in order to claim your prize

AMOE - Alternate Method of Entry or Alternate Means of Entry

ARV - Approximate Retail Value

CAPTCHA - Completely Automated Public Turing Test to tell Computers and Humans Apart

DOB - Date of Birth

E/F/A - Employees, Family, Agencies - This is generally listed concerning eligibility to enter

FB - Facebook

GC - Gift Certificate

GP - Grand Prize

IWG - Instant Win Game

MSRP - Manufacturer's Suggested Retail Price

NAZ - Name, Address, and Zip code

NAZT - Name, Address, Zip, Telephone Number

OEB - Official Entry Blank

OEF - Official Entry Form

OGP - Official Game Piece

P/H - Postage and Handling

POP - Proof of Purchase

RECV - Received by

ROM- Regardless of Method

SAE - Self-Addressed Envelope

SASE - Self-Addressed Stamped Envelope

SD - Start Date The official beginning date for the sweepstakes or contest

SNAIL Mail - A postal sweepstakes entry

SWEEPER - A person who enters sweepstakes

SWEEPING - The act of entering sweepstakes

TBA - To Be Announced

UPC - Universal Product Code

UPS - United Parcel Service

USPS - United States Postal Service

WL - Winners List

Final Thoughts

The vast majority of promotion industry leaders appear to be in agreement there will always be contests and sweepstakes. What will certainly change is method of entry, the prizes and logistics. Small changes will occur rapidly. For instance, you will likely see physical gift card prizes replaced by virtual ones. You will encounter more location based sweepstakes, and you will start to see the use of virtual reality. Regardless of the changes large or small that occur, the underlying concept the chance to win a dream won't change.

After spending decades in marketing at various times there

were pundits predicting the death of prize promotions. Likewise, more than 50 years ago the investigation (by Congress) of pre-selected sweepstakes an industry publication wrote, "...and our friends at the independent judging organization will soon find themselves looked on as dinosaur trainers. They better start creating resumes for a new day job."

Source: Investigation of "Preselected Winners" Sweepstakes Promotions. Hearings before the United States House Select Committee on Small Business, Subcommittee on Activities of Regulatory Agencies Relating to Small Business, Ninety-First Congress, first session, on Nov. 12-14, 1969

Not surprisingly within a matter of 24 months, the industry was back and booming. What changed was the type of sweepstakes.

The very same publication during the dot com explosion devoted an issue to marketing changes as commerce goes digital. They wrote, "...and I think we can safely assume the death of prize promotions." Nobody saw the internet explosion but in reality, all that has changed in prize offers is the method of entry. You can still win millions from Publishers Clearing House™, you just enter online instead of using an envelope.

No one can be 100 percent certain exactly how sweepstakes will change. Yet years ago when Jeffery Feinman was asked this very question of how people might enter sweepstakes in the future, he responded saying: "My grandchildren one day may enter by pressing a chip implanted in their arm." Needless to say this brought guffaws. Yet the truth now is one can now enter by pressing a chip on their wrist via their iPhone™.

The underlying motivation for sweeps and contests is part of the human psyche. Michael Brown, a psychologist said, "The three strongest words in the English language may well be love, free and win but not necessarily in that order."

The future will usher in different methods of entry as well as the type of prizes. Millennials like different things than Baby

Boomers. But what is not different is a desire for something beyond one's reach.

Sweepstakes attract attention! Richard Stein, a brand manager, said: "There are few things one can say about their product that is as exciting as, 'Win a million dollars from Crispy Chips.'"

Technology will continue to bring new opportunities for sweepstakes. Producing a video about a product as a contest requirement was nearly impossible a few short years ago. Now most people who have a cellphone can be their own movie-maker. In fact, producing your own commercial was a contest requirement in a recent Super-Bowl™ contest for Doritos™. The winner got $1,000,000!

Even for nonprofits new technology offers new sweepstakes opportunities. The Grammy™ Foundation recently had a clever fundraiser. An online and social media electronic mosaic was created. If you wanted to show your support, you donated only $1.00 to upload your photo or phrase to become part of the mosaic. Then you could easily share it with your friends via Facebook™. All those who participated were entered into a sweepstakes for a chance to win a trip to the Grammy Awards™. (You could also enter the drawing offline for free.) This ran for an entire year with many thousands participating in the mosaic. Perhaps more important it was done to attract and reach millennials—the up and coming givers. That's who nonprofits and marketers need to be targeting.

The underlying theory remains the same. Select prizes that remind entrants what you stand for and attract the people you seek. A perfect example has 20 years of success in sweepstakes. Aircraft Owners and Pilots Association (AOPA) consistently offers an aircraft grand prize for its all-pilot target audience. Michelle Peterson, AOPA's VP of Membership, cites this promotion as a proven strategy for growth, generating new memberships, increasing re-enrollments and elevating membership levels. She noted, "The airplane sweepstakes affords multiple levels of membership engagement. For some sweepstakes, we have involved members by asking them to choose a paint scheme or even inviting member input on what aircraft we should offer. Editorially, it's a win/win because our members enjoy reading about the plane and the winner. The aircraft sweepstakes has also shown up as a highlight in membership satisfaction surveys."

What has changed over 20 years? Only the method of entry. Traditionally sweepstakes solicitations were delivered almost exclusively by direct mail or in print advertising but no more. Now with most everyone having a limited attention span we need to add to the mix.

Many marketers are now supplementing traditional print and television advertising with email campaigns, banner ads, sponsored content on key websites, text message campaigns, and Facebook™ and Twitter™ announcements and much more. All this effort is being done to make it easy for a potential buyer to react quickly. These embellishments add marginally to a marketing budget but can generate substantial increases in the number of "brand registrations" in the mind of consumers.

Many companies now spend more advertising dollars on the internet than in print or television. Clorox™ already spends more than half of its massive advertising budget on the internet. And media strategy change is not limited to a few companies. Not long ago, Fortune™ magazine predicted social media expenditure would overtake advertising expenditure by 2020.

Business is in a state of flux. Procter & Gamble™ is generally considered the single most sophisticated of all marketers. Yet only recently did they realize they were being ripped off by social media and internet companies. They were paying for ads that never appeared, or never appeared anywhere useful.

Lotteries were successful in the 1800s, contests a powerhouse in the 1940s, gas station games changed petroleum retailing in the 1960s, and sweepstakes were the cornerstone of direct mail in the 1980s. In 2030, 2050 and even 3000 you can be certain there will be some opportunity to win a fabulous prize! The late, Cy Draddy, President and founder of the D. L. Blair Corporation (an independent judging organization) liked to say, "We are in the dream business. If you want to change human behavior just give them a chance to win a dream!"

Quotes to remember…

"I am a great believer in luck, and I find the harder I work, the more I have of it." - Thomas Jefferson

"Luck is what happens when preparation meets opportunity." - Seneca

Frequently Asked Questions

In preparation for this book, a questionnaire was sent to many individuals who had previously purchased one of the prior books authored by Jeffrey Feinman on the topic of sweepstakes asking the simple yet direct question of what of the previous chapters they liked the most. Surprisingly, the Q&A section was the most popular. Several people commented, "With Q&A I quickly read this section to find out things I need to know." Others wrote, "With Q&A I can save time and just read those questions that truly interest me." With that in mind this section has been greatly expanded and the specific questions have all been selected for one of the following reasons:

the ones that always seem to get asked;

are the most interesting; or

ones that have been answered incorrectly in other publications or frequently subject to misinformation.

Many questions could be answered with simply repeating the mantra of "read the rules." Also when it is stated to "follow the rules" the next comment readers often make is "that's common sense." Yet time after time numerous winning entries are disqualified because the entrant failed to follow the rules. This is true even among experienced sweepers.

In the computer/internet world a page listing Frequently Asked Questions is one way companies keep from having to engage in a great deal of correspondence. It works because 95 percent of questions (for any particular product, service, or business) are the same.

The questions here are listed below in no particular order. Every question won't be of interest or help to every reader. However, even the most avid sweeper, we believe, will find some new information or insight. Ultimately, what all the answers have in common is that we trust they will move you closer to our mutual objective. That is, to make you a winner!

Q. How many people in the United States participate in sweepstakes?

A. Prior research has estimated that slightly more than half of the population has participated in sweepstakes at some time. However, if you ask people you get a totally different answer. For some reason, many folks find it embarrassing to say they enter sweepstakes. A number of focus groups were conducted recently. Approximately nine out of 10 people in each group said (a) they have never entered a sweepstakes and (b) they never would. They thought they were a waste of time. The interesting fact is 100 percent of these people at these focus groups came from lists derived exclusively from sweepstakes entries.

Q. Should you enter a sweepstakes if the prize is not something you can use? Some people say you should only enter for prizes you want and others say you should enter everything. What do you think is correct?

A: The world has definitely changed. Now with eBay™, Craigslist ™ and other sites you can sell most anything of value. In fact, sometimes a prize of limited appeal may mean fewer entries; hence, a better chance to win. Unless

> you are a craftsman a gallon of varnish might be of limited
> interest. In fact, even if you are a craftsman, a single gallon
> of varnish may hardly be worth your time to enter. At
> first glance a set of power tools might not generate any
> sweepstakes fervor to an apartment dweller. However,
> knowing that it has a $2,500 retail value may make it
> worth reconsidering.

There are, a few caveats when considering a sweeps with no-interest (to you) prizes. First, make sure the prize would have a resale value. For example, a national brand of dog food recently ran a sweepstakes with one of the prizes being a year's supply of dog food. The rules clearly state the winner would receive 365 coupons (redeemable at any local supermarket) each for a free can of dog food. This would be an easy coupon to sell on eBay™ (and should bring top dollar). However, if the prize was actually cases of dog food, the cost of reshipping these would probably make selling these online cost prohibitive unless someone locally was able to pick them up. Second, are you eligible to win the prize? The fact that you don't have a dog still makes the prize resalable, however, if the rules state "this offer is only open to dog owners" you may have to prove that fact. If you are thinking that is just a detail, think again!

Several years ago we were the judging organization for sweepstakes that offered a car as the grand prize. In fact it was a fully loaded sports car with a sticker value of over $50,000. That prize would be simple to resell today, yesterday or even 20 years ago. However, the rules clearly stated "offer only open to individuals that are licensed drivers at the time of entry." The winner, a sweepstakes hobbyist, failed to read the rules. Before the prize was to be awarded they were required to send us a photo copy of their driver's license. The winner did not have a driver's license, in fact, they had never learned to drive. What followed was a flurry of letters in which they attempted to obtain the prize in their brother's name. Next, they wanted the prize awarded and/or the car in their father's name, a state trooper. When both "offers" failed they made a shameless call to the judging organization in which they offered our prize director $10,000 in cash. Sadly (for the first name drawn), we had to award the prize to the runner-up.

Finally, another point of consideration is realizing that not all prizes are legal to sell. A case in point happened when the Pennsylvania State Liquor Control Board conducted an in store sweepstakes. The prize was a 12-year-old bourbon that normally sells for over $250. The winner of the prize decided to list it on Craigslist™ for sale for $59. A representative from the State Liquor Control Board answered the ad agreeing to purchase the liquor. The winner was then informed it was illegal to sell liquor without a license and faced possible fines of up to $1,200!

Q. I keep reading that an advertiser can't require you to buy to enter a sweepstakes. Yet some companies run sweepstakes that do not allow online entries. You must enter by mail. Therefore, you need to spend money for postage to enter. Why isn't the cost of the stamp viewed as "consideration"? How is it legal?

A. Under the law that is referred to as "3rd party beneficiary." The revenue goes to the United States Post Office not the sweepstakes sponsor. The sponsor of the sweepstakes receives no benefit from you spending postage monies.

Q. Can sweepstakes require participants to complete a survey? Some people have said that they cannot as this would constitute 'consideration,' but it appears to me that companies like Alaska Airlines™ require the completion of a survey in their rules. When is the required completion of a survey legal?

A. Consideration is one of the elements in a lottery. So one must understand basic lottery law. A lottery has three elements: prize, chance and consideration. For a prize offer to be a legal one, elements must be removed. In a skill contest, chance is eliminated. In sweepstakes, the element eliminated is consideration (by offering the opportunity to enter without a purchase). Herein comes the difficulty. The legal definition of consideration is "Something of value given by both parties to a contract that induces them to enter into the agreement to exchange mutual performances." By definition you can see consideration is not necessarily money.

Most people understand a contract that reads, "Joe's Panting Service agrees to paint John Doe's house for $2500." However, it is just as much of a contract if we were to write, "Joe's Painting Service will paint John Doe's house in exchange for John Doe's Chevrolet™ Nova." In both cases services are performed (house painting) for consideration (something of value).

To answer your specific question both the state and the federal government have usually referred to this as incidental consideration. On the other hand, there was a sweepstakes operator in the late 1990s that required a completed 15-page questionnaire as a requirement of entry. He was charged with violating the lottery laws. This was pre-internet and his intention was to sell names and mailing addresses to companies interested in very specific information (derived from detailed personal questions).

The answer, therefore ... is how much effort is involved in the questionnaire. That is, are we speaking of three questions or a thousand? Several states, at various times, have suggested a store visit is consideration. Therefore, many sweepstakes operators offer a write-in alternative. Currently, at least two state attorney generals have concern that endorsements (e.g. clicking "Like" on Facebook™) may be a sufficient consideration as to make a particular sweepstakes illegal.

Q. If you can't require purchase how is the 2016 Cheetos™ Weird Shape offer not illegal? Obviously, to find the weird shape you must buy. So I don't understand how with a requisite purchase necessary this is not a lottery? To me it looks like prize, chance and consideration are all present.

A. Once again we say the big secret is always ... read the rules. It is not illegal. If you read rule #6 you are advised (in part) "...To participate in the Contest without making a purchase, visit the website, view the gallery of Cheetos™ snacks, choose any Cheetos™ snack and follow the online instructions to provide a description of Cheetos™ snack you selected (also a "Contest Entry") and submit your Contest Entry as instructed.." Therefore buyers and non-buyers have the same chance of winning. To understand if an offer is a lottery, which is illegal unless run by the state, (which must have prize, chance and consideration present) just read the rules and look for the method of entry without purchase.

Q. How will I know if I won the sweepstakes? The rules state that winners would be contacted by phone. I got a call from an unknown number in Colorado and the phone only rang for a few seconds. Was it them? How will I know if it's them? What number will they use? Will they ring for a few seconds then hang up or let it ring all the way through?

A. It's very unusual for winners to be notified by phone. However, if this is a legitimate sweepstakes and you are in fact a winner, they will make a reasonable attempt to reach you. That is, calling numerous times and letting the phone ring until it is answered. If you have an answering machine, they will leave a message.

Q. Have you ever won any kind of sweepstakes or contest?

A. Yes. Although individuals are not allowed to enter sweepstakes or contest when you are involved its design or administration. However, both authors have entered and won sweepstakes and/or contests conducted by others.

Q. In a sweepstakes, how do you win a lifetime supply of something?

A. Just look for a sweepstakes in which the prize is "a lifetime supply of ..." It may be hard to find as companies know $100,000, a new car or a trip will appeal to more people than a lifetime supply of something. Sweepstakes prizes are designed to appeal to potential customers.

Q. Given I live in a state with a high income tax is entering sweepstakes really worth it? If I won cash prizes, a car, or a house...wouldn't I have to pay for taxes for it? Wouldn't that make it pointless then and just financially hard? Might it even move me into another tax bracket?

A. The taxes are a percentage of fair market value. That is, you could sell your prize and the taxes would never be more than half of what you collected (depending on your tax bracket). If your tax bracket moves up, it doesn't affect your initial earnings. On the additional earnings, your prize, you would not pay more than 50 percent and it might be much less. Yes, it's worth entering, unless you know someplace else to get travel, trips and cash for free!

Q. I have an idea that if I concentrate on one sweepstakes I am likely to win. That is, instead of sending 10 entries to 100 different sweepstakes I am better off sending 1,000 entries to 1 sweepstakes. Isn't a 1,000 entries a huge amount of entries and enough to assure me that I will win a prize?

A. A thousand entries may be a lot of entries. It depends what sweepstakes. Some sweepstakes only get a total of one thousand entries yet others get millions. The other problem is if you are entering a mail-in sweepstakes. To mail 1,000 entries using an envelope would (currently) cost $490 in postage. There is no guarantee you will win a prize but even if you did win you need to look at the value of the prizes. Recently, a sweepstakes offered 1,000 Timex watches as prizes; there is one prize to a family. It's projected by the sponsor that they will get only a few thousand entries. In this sweeps your chance to win would be great but, of course, it makes no sense to spend $490 in postage to win a $39 watch.

Q. What are my chances of winning a high-value raffle/drawing/giveaway in my life?

A. It depends on a number of factors. The main ones being (a) how often do you enter (b) which do you enter (some have many entrants some have a few) (c) are they legit... the vast majority of prize promotions are honest but some smaller offers are frauds (d) how much are you willing to spend. Although you can enter online sweepstakes for free, mail-in entries cost postage, and some raffle tickets are very expensive (e) how many entries do you place in each offer; although some sweepstakes are one entry to a family some allow unlimited entries, I have seen individuals that have entered a single prize promotion over 5,000 times. Assuming you did the most of all of these (e.g. made entering a full-time job and spent thousands of dollars and thousands of hours each year entering) I would say your chance of winning is significant. You will meet people who will say, "I think those things are fixed. Nobody in my family has ever won." When you ask them how often they enter they then will remark, "Oh we never enter."

Q. What are the best ways, aside from Google™, to find photography contests to enter? I'm on websites like Gurushots™, and Viewbug™, etc., but I'm searching for a schedule/calendar of upcoming photography contests to enter. Are there any maintained lists or calendars to refer to?

A. Photo contests are most often conducted by photo equipment manufacturers and travel related products and magazines. Register at sites of such firms. Additionally, photo magazines often conduct photo contests in both consumer and trade photo publications. You may subscribe to Rangefinder™ (a free publication for professionals) if you are a professional photographer. They normally offer one or more contests every month. If you can prove you are a professional apply for a free trade subscription to Rangefinder™. Some months they will have four or five contests. In addition, photo contests are often annual events. Check companies that previously ran such contests.

Q. I asked Publishers Clearing House™ how they fund their sweepstakes, I got a response, but I don't understand it completely? They said: "Our $10 million and $1 million prizes are generally funded by securities held by an independent agent. These securities generate interest which is paid semi-annually to the winner." What about the $5,000 a week for life and similar prizes? Who is the "Independent Agent" in this context? What are the "Securities" in this context and how do they generate interest?

A. Most often these type of programs are funded through an insurance company. One simply buys a single pay annuity. Not much different than if you went to an insurance broker when you retired and bought a policy that paid you $1,000 a month as long as you live. Only difference of course, PCH™ or whoever is buying a much larger policy with a much higher premium because of the (a) age of the winner and (b) the amount of the policy.

Q. Is there any evidence that Publisher's Clearing House™ yearly awards someone $5,000 a week "forever?"

A. Absolutely. Publishers Clearing House™ in fact may be one of the single most investigated corporations in America. They have had inquiry from both federal and state regulators. Yet they were never found to not award a prize. The company is absolutely legitimate. An interesting side note is that in their history they have contributed hundreds of millions of dollars to charity.

Q. What is the largest prize awarded by the Publishers Clearing House™ sweepstakes to a non-purchaser?

A. PCH™ does not publish a winners list by buyers or non-buyers. However, based on both PCH's™ own data and published data (based on federal and state inquiries) the majority of major prize winners have been non-buyers. As with most mail-in offers, there are more entries from non-buyers than buyers. Therefore, it is statistically correct that more prizes would go to non-buyers.

Q. How do decorated envelopes give you an advantage to winning if prize winners are drawn by blindfolded judges?

A. Great question. Let me explain. Yes, major prizes and grand prizes are frequently drawn with the judge being blindfolded. However, most sweepstakes have numerous prizes. If the runner up prizes (for example) were 10 computers and 100 gift certificates and 1,000 watches and 10,000 coupons for free candy bars it would be impractical to do such drawings blindfolded. Although major prizes are drawn by senior staff the runner up prizes are most often drawn by others at a junior level. When Mr. Feinman was running an independent judging organization, he recalled one year where they had well over three dozen sweepstakes close December 31st. These sweepstakes were comprised of over 50,000 prizes! As you might imagine a person spending their entire day drawing out winning entries can get quite boring. You can train individuals to just draw at random, but human beings act like human beings. It does not take much imagination to realize that out of the boredom often comes a desire to add some excitement to the day. An envelope with stickers and Day-Glo ink that stands out is more likely to be picked than just one more boring business size envelope. There are many sweepstakes hobbyist that make envelopes from everything from old maps to cut up fabric. Most are carefully made to make sure they meet the required measurement of a business (#10) envelope. In short, a clever design might not get you the $100,000 grand prize, but it might help win a TV set or a computer!

Q. I've heard companies keep lists of people who enter lots of sweepstakes. Is that true?

A. No. It's not. If they did, what could they do with the list?

Q. My second cousin works for an independent judging organization. When I see, "Not open to members of immediate
family," does that mean I can't enter their sweepstakes?

A. Immediate family means any of the following: spouse, ex-
spouse, de facto spouse, child or step child, parent, step
parent, grandparent, step grandparent, uncle, aunt, niece,
nephew, brother, sister, step brother, step sister or first cousin.

Q: Why do sponsors prefer printing to cursive when filling out
3"x 5" cards or papers?

A: Judges have found that the majority of handwritten entries
are poor. Therefore, they ask for printing which is almost
always easier to read.

Q. Are there any new scams to watch out for?

A. There are many new ones, but the red flag is always the
same-a request for money. No legitimate sweepstakes
will ever ask you to pay anything to obtain your prize.
However, crooks become more brazen. Recently, one con
man actually bought names of sweepstakes entrants and
then showed up in a brown uniform (similar to UPS) and
actually rang people's door bells. He explained he was with
the shipping company for a major sweepstakes company
and they needed to verify the address. He wanted
to "arrange for delivery of your big screen TV, Apple™
computer, and iPhone™"; he then asked for a check for the
shipping. Needless to say anyone that gave him a check
never saw any prizes or the money again.

Another con happened right after Christmas. A team of
swindlers worked their way thru several small towns in Northern
Indiana. They rented a truck and painted it "Prize Patrol™." You
can guess what came next.

Also, there was a report of another group of shameless
scoundrels operating out of California. These villains actually have
the nerve to use the name of the Federal Trade Commissioner.

Here's how they operate.

It starts with a letter from a lawyer in California. He says the FTC appointed him to notify you about a claim [spoiler: he didn't], and includes a letter from FTC Commissioner Joshua Wright enlisting his help [spoiler: it's fake]. The letter says you entered a sweepstakes and won $2.5 million, but you didn't claim your prize so it was forfeited. But thanks to an FTC investigation into sweepstakes companies, you have a chance to claim your $2.5 million prize. Sure, you could claim it on your own. Or, you could do it the "cheaper, faster, and completely painless" way — hire this firm to help you. If you read the detailed retainer agreement that you are asked to sign, you'll see it will cost you thousands. The whole story is made up. No prize. No FTC case. But it can be tricky to tell. The scammer includes actual FTC advice and throws in legal-sounding phrases. But the only thing he really wants is your money! Some scammers tell pretty good lies, mixing in truth to make them stick. Here are some facts you can bank on:

No FTC Commissioner or staff is involved in giving out sweepstakes prizes.

The FTC doesn't oversee sweepstakes. However, they do go after sweepstakes scams.

No company, state or federal government agency will ask you for money to claim a prize.

If you enter and win a legitimate sweepstakes, you don't have to pay insurance, taxes, or shipping charges to collect your prize. If you have to pay, it's not a prize.

If an FTC case has resulted in refunds, you can find the details at: https://www.ftc.gov/enforcement/cases-proceedings/refunds.

Q. I know Publishers Clearing House ™ runs the biggest sweepstakes. Who runs the biggest contest?

A. Pillsbury™ a division of General Mills™ run the biggest contest. The Pillsbury™ bake-off is the granddaddy (or grandmother) of all contests. It actually dates back to

1949. After World War II the country was busy celebrating. Suddenly sugar rations were over and housewives were clipping recipes from magazines. Adversity had changed to prosperity. The marketing folks did not want to miss out on this opportunity. The people of Pillsbury™ decided to run the biggest contest ever. The biggest contest is exactly what they did. They kicked off a campaign with a huge advertising budget. They brought the finalists to the famous Waldorf-Astoria™ in New York for a PR event still unmatched. Philip Pillsbury, the president of the company at that time, told the marketing people to do everything first class. And so they did! The finalists were served breakfast in bed and pampered as they were accompanied around New York in the style usually reserved for heads of state.

At the first bake-off was former First Lady Anna Roosevelt, as well as radio celebrity Art Linkletter. The event was covered like it was the Academy Awards™. The host was the then famous personality, Arthur Godfrey.

Although the names change, the fanfare changes very little. A hundred finalists are flown to a special site where they are greeted like superstars. There are gala breakfasts, lunches and dinners where they meet the fellow contestants and celebrities. It's a magical contest weekend. And it's still a PR dream for the Pillsbury™ Company.

The day of the final bake-off the hundred finalists walk in as the band plays "As the Saints Come Marching In." The host has included a cross-section of celebrities from Martha Stewart to Marie Osmond. Even the announcement of winners is an event unto itself. Recently the winner was announced on the Food Network™, in 2010 the winners were on the Oprah Winfrey show and most recently the grand prize recipient appeared on the Martha Stewart show.

Obviously, your next question is how do you win? Perhaps not surprisingly the instructions are much the same the first and most important thing is to follow rules. This particular contest offering has more than a staggering number of entries. And because it has so many first time entrants a huge number are disqualified simply because they did not follow the rules. This usually manifests itself by the recipe not being original, failure to list specific ingredients, and with the biggest cause of failure, forgetting to include the sponsor's product in the ingredients! In the original 1949 contest the only requirement was a cup of Pillsbury™ flour. More recently, as the Pillsbury™ family of brands has grown so has the list of qualifiers. The family now includes Green Giant™ frozen vegetables, Crisco™, Watkins Vanilla™, Häagen-Dazs™ ice cream and Yoplait™ yogurt to name a few. In addition to the number of categories growing, so has the number of special imagination awards. No doubt Philip Pillsbury would not have imagined the special Pillsbury™ gluten-free award or the Reynolds Baking Magic Award™. As American tastes change so have the winning recipes. Pillsbury™ even amended the rules to allow men to enter. Much of the popularity of this contest relates its reflection of everyday tastes rather than recipes that might appear in fancy restaurants. The idea always has been to have this be a cross-section of American taste. Truly what America is eating!

Q: Which is easier to win - a sweepstakes or contest?

A: It depends. Most people think it's easier to win a contest because there are usually far fewer entries. However, if your culinary skills are like those of the authors, it's unlikely you will be winning any cooking contests. Contests require skill to win. Therefore, enter contests in an area that you are good at. The very same person that finds recipe contests easy might find essay contests nearly impossible. Assuming you have a particular skill you may find contests are the route to winning. Contests get a fraction of the entries that sweepstakes get.

Q: I enter so many sweepstakes online! I know I have made a mistake and entered more than once in a sweepstakes that the rules state one per person. What should I do? Will the sponsor or judging agency really know?

A: They may, but there is nothing you can do now. Just be more careful the next time.

Q: Why does the sponsor want me to "Like" them on Facebook™? What does it matter?

A: Some marketers feel that many "Likes" indicate a popular product. Therefore, if you "Like" a product your friends might be encouraged to try it. The entire area of social media is so new that many advertisers are still on the learning curve and have yet to test some theories. There has not been any definitive proof given that Facebook™ "Likes" translate directly into improving one's business in most product categories.

Q: The sponsor's online entry form has a box to check to send me more promotional email. Are my odds of winning better if I check the box?

A: No. Your odds are the same if you check or don't check that box.

Q: Is it ok if I use RoboForm™ to help fill out my online entry?

A: Absolutely. And it will save lots of time.

Q: If a sweepstakes has only a few prizes offered should I skip entering that because the odds of winning those are less?

A: Not necessarily. The odds of winning depend on how many entries are received. The number of prizes is just one of many factors as to the number of entries that will be competing.

Q: If I cannot find the official rules listed is the sweepstakes a scam?

A: No. There is no legal requirement a sponsor list rules with every ad.

Q: Is it a requirement by law that ALL sweepstakes have to post the official rules?

A: They don't need to always post them everywhere they advertise they just need to have them available.

Q: Is it legal for a sweepstakes to credit more entries to those that buy something from their website versus those that might send in a free alternative means of entry?

A: No. Buyers and non-buyers must have the same chance of winning.

Q: Why do most sweepstakes not allow you to use a post office box as an address?

A: Prizes are frequently shipped by United Parcel Service (UPS). Some will ship by Federal Express. Very large prizes may be shipped by a freight carrier. The post office only allows post office box holders to receive mail and packages that have been sent through the United States Postal Service (USPS).

Q: I read in the rules that only one entry is allowed per envelope. Is there a specific reason why multiple entries are not allowed in the envelopes?

A: Yes. Most sweepstakes winners are drawn from sealed envelopes. The thought is why go to the expense of opening up thousands (or even millions) of envelopes. After the winning envelopes are drawn they are then opened to (a) see if they comply with the rules and (b) to obtain the name and address of the entrants. If you could mail multiple entries in one envelope the judging organization would have to open all then envelopes to include all entries.

Q: What is the difference between these words in the rules: "a sheet of paper," "a piece of paper," "a card"?

A: When the rules say you should use a sheet of paper, this means use a piece of standard size paper without lines.

A standard-size sheet of paper measure 8 $\frac{1}{2}$ by 11 inches and folds for a standard-size envelope. This means that a legal sheet or piece of paper torn from a legal pad is not acceptable. A piece of paper can mean almost any size unless a certain size is specified. The usual size specified is 3" x 5" and you can substitute a standard blank index card, if you wish. However, if the rules specify a 3" x 5" card, don't substitute a piece of paper. Cards are sturdier, don't crease as easily, and often pass through the mail with less wear-and-tear. This generally means the judges can read entries from cards easier.

Q: What does the sponsor mean when he says he wants you to print your entry on a plain 3" x 5" sheet of paper?

A: This means that in this case, 3" x 5" is the only size acceptable and the paper or card should not be ruled.

Q: If the rules call for a 3"x 5" piece of paper is using a 3"x 5" card ok?

A: Yes, a 3"x 5" card is paper. On the other hand if the rules call for a 3"x 5" card don't use a piece of paper. Although a card is paper; a paper is not a card!

Q: If I use variations of my name like: Susan Jones, Susan P. Jones, or Priscilla Jones to enter a sweepstakes is that ok?

A: Sure. That is unless the rules say print your full name or given name. In such a case you would, of course, print your full name or given name.

Q: If the rules state that a person can only win one prize but his/her name is actually drawn as a winner for multiple prizes how do you determine which prize they receive?

A: It depends the order in which the prizes are drawn. As soon as your name is drawn that is the prize you win. If the judging organization draws the grand prize first and works down you are in luck. However, if they work in reverse and your name is drawn for the pen and pencil set you are out of luck if subsequently your name is drawn for the million dollar grand prize.

Q: Can the outer envelope address be typed and generated by a computer?

A: It depends. If the rules say (and they usually do) hand print your entry you would be disqualified if any part of your entry was computer printed.

Q: Does it matter if my entry envelope has my return address on it?

A: No. Unless in the official rules it is required by the sponsor.

Q: If the sweepstakes asks for my home phone, and I give them a cell number, will I be disqualified?

A: It depends. If that is your home number, it's not a problem.

Q: I am concerned about identity theft. If I give a fake date of birth, and I win, will I be disqualified?

A: You certainly could be. Again, you must follow the rules.

Q: Do judging agencies have a black list of people who win a lot of prizes?

A: No. If they did how could these people win lots of prizes?

Q: I read a lot about sweepers staggering mail-in entries, does this effect my odds of winning any?

A: No, it doesn't.

Q: Do different size envelopes affect my odds of it getting drawn from the mail bag?

A: Yes. It might reduce your odds to zero if the rules say "enter using a #10 business envelope." On the other hand, if there is no reference to the size envelope, a large envelope will increase your chance of winning (if the judging organization draws from a sealed envelope).

Q: Are entries drawn from the envelopes out of a mail bag or are they drawn from the 3" x 5" qualifier or none of the above?

A: Usually from envelopes.

Q: Why are judging agencies so secretive?

A: They want everyone to have the same chance to win. Giving someone special information might increase their chance to win.

Q: Does flooding mail entries toward the end of the promotion help me have better odds of winning?

A: No.

Q: Are decorated envelopes picked more as winners than non-decorated envelopes?

A: Yes. Although major prizes are drawn by someone blindfolded minor prizes are drawn by clerks who may be drawn to decorated envelopes.

Q: I know I should not use a pencil when filling out entries. Is there a certain color pen that is preferred? Does it have to be blue or black ink or does it matter?

A: No. It doesn't matter.

Q: On average how many entries are disqualified in a sweepstakes drawing?

A: It depends on the number of entries received.

Q: What are the top three reasons entries are disqualified?

A: They didn't follow the rules. In some cases they entered late, wrong address, wrong size envelope, wrong size qualifier and every other violation of the rules.

Q: Is it acceptable to use as your address a business address?

A: It depends. If the rules state one entry to a household than, you must use either but not both. If it asks for your home address, it's not acceptable.

Q: Should I expect more junk mail because I enter sweepstakes?

A: Usually not. However, with some online sweepstakes it will increase your spam mail.

Q: What exactly does the sponsor or judging agency do with the mail in entries the day they arrive?

A: Stack them up in mail bags.

Q: How big is a mail bag?

A: Mailbags come in various sizes.

Q: Who picks the winning entries? Is the person really blindfolded?

A: Usually an official of the judging organization will draw major prizes and he (or she) is really blindfolded. Minor prizes are drawn by clerks.

Q: I don't like giving out my social security number to anyone. Do I have to if I win a prize?

A: Yes. Legally you can't be awarded a prize of $600 unless the sponsor has your social security number.

Q: I won a gift card worth $1,000. Why does an affidavit need to be filled out?

A: To make sure you complied with the rules.

Q: I won a trip for two and it requires me to have my guest sign a waiver. Why is that necessary?

A: For the same reason you must sign one. To protect the sponsor from being sued.

Q: When I win sometimes I see that my prize comes from a "prize fulfillment center." What exactly is that?

A: Usually a large warehouse where prizes are stored and subsequently shipped.

Q: Should I use a #10 envelope or are any size envelopes ok?

A: Again, read the rules.

Q: Are bright color envelopes better to use versus just a plain white envelope?

A: Same as decorated envelopes.

Q: The sweepstakes rules specify using a "standard postcard." What does that mean?

A: A postcard printed and sold by the United States Post Office.

Q: Does adding lots of stamps to my envelope help it stand out to help me win more?

A: Sometimes. It's the same theory as decorated envelopes.

Q: If I use a postage machine to stamp my entries is that acceptable?

A: Again, read the rules. It may say add first class stamps. In that case a postage meter is not acceptable.

Q: The rules of the sweepstakes show: "Win Jones Sausages," PO Box 156, Baltimore, MD 21023. Does this mean I need to write the quotes as part of the entry?

A: No.

Q: Can I use a sticker for my return address on the outer envelope? Does it matter?

A: You can unless the rules ask for the return address to be hand written.

Q: Is it ok to put stickers or glitter on the outside of my envelope or postcard entry?

A: It's fine and it might just help. But it could get jammed and torn when being processed by the post office as well.

Q: Is there an advantage to making my entry envelope heavier by stuffing it with additional paper?

A: Yes. Anything that makes it stand out may help, but it might also get you disqualified depending on the judging agency and of course what is listed in the official the rules.

Q: If I am concerned that I might miss the drawing, can I send my entry by priority mail?

A: Again, check the rules. It will usually say enter by first class mail.

Q: How many entries have you ever seen one person enter in a sweepstakes? Did they win?

A: 5,000. Yes. They won but all minor prizes, each was worth less than $25.

Q: What is the least number of entries you have seen a promotion receive?

A: 35. Fortunately, there were only 25 prizes.

Q: How long do you wait after the sweepstakes is completed to do the drawings?

A: The next day.

Q: I won a television but really don't need a television. Would a sponsor ever consider giving me cash instead?

A: No. Frequently the sponsor gets very good prizes because of the advertising value of the sweepstakes. Of course, you can always sell the TV.

Q: A few times when I mailed off a postcard, the post office mailed it back to me. Is it ok to write my information on the diagonal so it won't be confused with the delivery address?

A: Yes. That is fine.

Q: What is the difference between the sponsor, the independent judging agency, and the advertising company?

A: The sponsor is the company that owns the original product. This product is the reason for the sweepstakes. The sweepstakes is created to promote the product or service to the buying public. The sponsor usually hires a promotion company or an advertising company to give advice in the promotion of the product and to devise the sweepstakes or contest. The promotion company or the sponsor hires an independent judging organization to handle the mechanics of the contest, the drawings as well as the awarding of prizes.

Q: If I win, when and how will I find out about it?

A: This varies from company to company, from sweepstakes to sweepstakes. Often, many companies notify the grand prize winners right away. Lesser winners may have to wait several months while the judging organization double-checks winning entries to make sure the information was filled out properly. Most companies try to take care of these details as fast as possible. They know you are excited, and of course they are happy to give you your prize. You may be notified by email, phone or by mail. Form letters are very much alike. Usually, only the size and nature of the prize differs from letter to letter.

Q: If I win, do I need to thank the sponsor for my prize?

A: You don't have to. You might be inclined to. It might be fun to sit down and write a thank-you note. After all, when someone gives you a gift, you perform this simple kindness. It makes the giver feel good. And it probably makes you feel good.

Q: I recently won a trip to go to a concert, but I can't get the time off to go. Is it ok to let my brother go in my place?

A: Again those magic words" follow the rules." Frequently, the rules will state prizes are not transferable. However, if it's not stated once you win a prize, be it tickets or a TV, you are free to sell it, give it away or keep it.

Q: If I am notified that I won a prize, but it never arrives whom should I contact?

A: You should contact the person who notified you. If you don't get a satisfactory response notify the sponsor.

Q: If I win a prize am I obligated to accept it?

A: No.

Q: What should I do if I can't pay the taxes on the prize I won?

A: The same thing if you can't pay your taxes for any reason. Speak with an accountant or contact the IRS. Of course, you can sell your prize and use that money to pay the tax and in most cases you will have additional money left over.

Q: If I was notified that I won a large prize of $5,000 in December, but I did not actually get the check until January, when are taxes due?

A: Ask your accountant or the IRS.

Q: I won a prize package and the sponsor sent me a 1099-M Form that said it was worth $12,500. I need to sell it to pay the taxes and only sold it for $5,700 now what do I do?

A: Contact the sponsor and the IRS. Your liability is a fair market value of the prize. If $5,700 was the most you could get then that will be your tax liability. Sometimes the sponsor will just provide you with an amended 1099. Regardless the IRS will consider your position and if the price you got was fair then that will be the amount on which you were taxed. The problems come in when someone wins a Lexus™ and tries to get away with selling it to their brother for $500. Don't try it ... you won't win. And then you not only will have to pay the tax but interest and penalties.

Q: Can a non US owned company host a contest or sweepstakes in the United States?

A: This is not a problem as long as they follow US regulations (filings, bonds, lottery, etc.). Any number of major prize promotions are conducted in the USA by foreign companies. In fact Unilever™ is Swiss owned and for many years was a major user of prize promotions as a marketing vehicle.

Q: Can you reuse a stamp from a mailed letter that did not get postmarked?

A: No, absolutely not! According to 18 U.S.C. § 1720, paragraph 3, Whoever knowingly uses in payment of postage, any postage stamp, postal card, or stamped envelope, issued in pursuance of law, which has already been used for a like purpose -- Shall be fined under this title or imprisoned not more than one year, or both.

Q. Why are lotteries considered bad?

A. Your chance to win is miniscule. They usually take money from the people that can afford it the least (the poor). If you want to throw down a buck and have some fun so be it. The bad comes in when you see unemployed and poor folks putting hundreds of dollars into lottery tickets with some fantasy that this is the way out of their troubles. (It's not).

Q: Why are lotteries won so frequently and within a short amount of time if the probability of winning is so low?

A: Simply because of the number playing. Your chance of winning is very, very small. The chance of SOMEONE winning is great. Simple math. If your chance of winning is one in ten million if 10 million people play, someone will win.

Q. How does the Powerball™ lottery work?

A. The "magic" to Powerball™ is the big prize. The game is played in 44 states, the District of Columbia, Puerto Rico and the US Virgin Islands - all generating the revenue - and adding to the prize fund. Hence, a huge grand prize. With 44 state residents adding to a prize fund the prize is gigantic. Non-residents of the 44 states can still legally play, but they must physically go to one of those states to buy tickets. Tickets must be purchased with cash. The specifics are the player picks five numbers between 1 and 59. Then the player picks a Powerball™ number between 1 and 35. Players can select these numbers, or they can choose "quick pick" which allows the computer to pick the numbers. Twice a week numbers are selected on TV.

To win "simply"...

Match 5 numbers and the Powerball™ number = Jackpot
Match 5 numbers, not including the Powerball™ number = $1 million dollars
Match 4 numbers and the Powerball™ number = $10,000
Match 4 numbers, not including the Powerball™ number = $100
Match 3 numbers and the Powerball™ number = $100
Match 3 numbers, not including the Powerball™ number = $7
Match 2 numbers and the Powerball™ number = $7
Match 1 number and the Powerball™ number = $6
Match only the Powerball™ number = $4

Q. What is the material used to make the silver scratch-off area on prepaid cards and lottery tickets?

A. Various materials are used depending on who is printing. They range from simply silver colored ink mixes with a latex base to much more sophisticated materials.

Q. Why do most winning scratch off lottery tickets come from gas stations and small stores?

A. Prizes are distributed at the same ratio as tickets are sold. More winners come from small stores simply because more lottery tickets are sold in small stores than large stores.

Q. Is it true that winning lottery tickets expire if they are not claimed within a certain time? Have there ever been big lottery prizes that went unclaimed?

A. Yes. Winning lottery tickets must be claimed with a certain time period and many go unclaimed. Usually the winner has one year to claim the prize but state laws vary. As of the publication of this book the biggest unclaimed jackpot on record is a $77 million prize that was won in Georgia in 2011. Just this year California had a $63 million winner who never came forward. (That's in spite of the state issuing press releases giving the exact date and location where the winning ticket was sold.) California previously had a $28 million jackpot that went unclaimed. Back in 2002 an Indiana lottery ticket worth $51 million went unclaimed. Of course, there are many, many small prizes that are never awarded. In the aggregate there is well over a billion dollars in unclaimed prizes every year.

A favorite last minute claim story come from Iowa. Two days after Christmas in 2011, a ticket worth $16.5 million was turned in just two hours before the Iowa Lottery deadline!

There are also occasions where the winner did show up too late to claim his/her prize. Recently, one woman came forward three years too late. In other cases a week or two late. And Clarence Jackson Jr. won the Connecticut Lotto back in 1996 but showed up just three days after the deadline. Mr. Jackson had a year to claim his winnings, but was busy taking care of his sick parent and supposedly said, "I just didn't have time to pick up the winnings." He tried to "cut a deal" to get a portion of the money. They refused to give him a dime.

In many European countries, unclaimed prizes are donated to charity. In the United States, any monies not awarded goes right back into the state coffers. As you might imagine state officials will not bend the rules. In fact, a California official was quoted as saying, "The State may have really hit the jackpot." That was just two weeks after the largest lotto prize ever ($648 million) still hadn't had the winner come forward. Alas, the winner was just meeting with lawyers to discuss his options./

There are any number of reasons why prizes go unclaimed; it's often not just lost or misplaced tickets. There actually tend to be more unclaimed prizes in the super prize games. When someone enters to win a huge prize, and see they didn't hit the jackpot they often don't check to see if they won any smaller prizes. In a one billion dollar game, recently several folks who saw they didn't win the super-prize just tore up their ticket. In that case, many smaller prizes (some of over a million dollars) went unclaimed!

Q. When will the next billion-dollar jackpot happen in the lottery?

A. Impossible to tell. It depends how many weeks it is until there is a lottery winner. When there is no grand prize winner in a lottery the prize rolls over and dollars are added. That grand prize keeps growing. However, for it to reach a billion it means the lottery needs to go many weeks without a winner. On the other hand, it is surprising the interest in that big number. Research shows there are people that will not play at $90 million but will stand on line for hours at $100 million. One might wonder why people feel as if $90 million isn't enough?

Q: I have noticed that some online sweepstakes sites require me to watch a video that lasts thirty seconds or sometimes longer than a minute before I can enter the sweepstakes. Is this legal?

A: I assume you are referring to the legal requirement that a sweepstakes must eliminate the element of "consideration." You are correct that consideration need not be money but could be time. However, it's been held that "incidental time" is not consideration. That is, the time you spend addressing an envelope, answering a short question or watching a short video would not be "consideration." However, if you had to watch a full-length movie the sponsor would legally be required to let you enter without watching the entire film.

Q: What does daily entry mean? Does it mean I can enter every 24 hours or does it mean if I enter at 5:00 p.m. on one day that I have to wait until 5:00 p.m. the next day in order to enter?

A: Unless specified in the rules, it means calendar date. That is, you can answer once on July 3, once on July 4th, once on July 5th and so on. The trap here is do the rules refer to business days, in which case the answer is different.

Q: If the sweepstakes allows you to enter daily, how do I figure out the time zone where the sweepstakes is running to know when I can enter the following day?

A: Again read the rules. If not indicated, it is once a day in your time zone.

Q: What does the term weekly entry mean? Once every seven days, or Sunday to Sunday?

A: A calendar week.

Q: Why do sweepstakes ask for my date of birth?

A: Two reasons. First, the Children's Online Privacy Protection Rule was developed and enacted by Congress in 2000 (amended 2012). The Rule was designed to protect children under age 13. The Rule prohibits operators of commercial websites and online services (including mobile apps) collect, use, or disclose personal information from children under the age of 13. Any information derived from a sweepstakes entrant under the age of 13 (including his/her name and address) violates the law. Fines for violating the law are huge. One marketer who collected only 1,000 entries faced fines that exceeded 40 million dollars. Second, some sweepstakes limit entries to individuals above the age of 60, housewives 18 to 39, etc. Asking for a date of birth assures compliance.

Q: I have been told that having an email address like sweeper-pro@gmail.com or iwanttowin@hotmail.com is not a good idea because it identifies me as someone who likes to enter sweepstakes. Does this hurt my chances of winning, is that true?

A: Technically it should not but to be on the safe side you might want to consider not using those types of identifiers in your email address.

Q: How are mail-in entries and electronic entries treated the same?

A: It varies. The most common method is a random selection. If for example there were 10 online entries for every mail-in entry a typical procedure is called "index carding." Simply put the judging organization would use a random number table and select 1,000 potential winners from the online entries. These 1,000 entries would then be entered on a database and printed out one to an index card. Then 100 mail-in entries would be selected. They would be opened and those that correctly entered (following the rules) would be entered on index cards. Additional entries would be drawn in each case until there were 10,000 correctly entered online entries and 1.000 corrected entered mail-in entries. All 11,000 index cards would be combined in a large drum and winners selected by random drawing.

Q: How do I figure out the odds of winning a sweepstakes?

A: It varies with the type of sweepstakes, but in a typical mail in sweepstakes the chance of winning is a function of how many total entries were received as well as how many times you entered and how many prizes total. For example, there was a sweepstakes in which 100,000 entries were received and you entered once, and assuming one prize you have one chance in 100,000 to win. If you entered twice you would have one chance in 50,000. Yes, just by entering twice you doubled your chance to win!

Q: Is it ok to mail in my entry before the official start date?

A: No. Again, given you failed to follow the rules, your entry would be disqualified. Many times sponsors don't even open the post office box for receipt until the start date. For example, if the start date was July 1st and you sent in entries in June there is every possibility those early entries will be discarded.

Q: Why do I sometimes see different addresses for the same sweepstakes in different advertisements?

A: Advertisers will use different post office boxes to determine what media produces the greatest number of entries. Although that information may interest a sponsor, the address you respond to does not affect your chance to win.

Q: If the rules say one entry per household, can I use my home address to enter and also use my mother's home address to enter too?

A: Not unless you enter under your mother's name. You can only have a single household.

Q: I recently won a trip to go to a concert, but I can't get the time off to go. Is it ok to let my brother go in my place?

A: Once again...depends on the rules. Sometimes the rules will say "ticket prizes are non-transferable." Assuming there is no reference to "prize transferable," you are free to send to your brother, sell your tickets or give them away. It's just as if you won a computer or a TV. In most cases once you win the prize you can do with it whatever you choose.

If you have any questions or comments feel free to contact either Jeffrey Feinman feinman@consultant.com or John Minges john@minges.com.

You can also find us online at www.SweepstakesExpert.com.

Made in United States
Orlando, FL
12 March 2023